THE FAITH
BETWEEN US

CONTENTS

FOREWORD

— *Stephen J. Dubner* —

RELIGION, IT STRIKES ME, has been hijacked by the *noisy*. Where are all the sincere, wise, good-hearted people who live each day in quiet pursuit of answers (or perhaps questions) as to how we should live on earth, and to what measure that life should include some sort of God?

If you watch the news on television or read a newspaper or trudge into the blogosphere, you might have no idea that such creatures still exist. The public face of religion is set in a deep scowl. Most public discussions of religion these days center on some standoff or misdeed, be it theological or political or sexual; the only voices making themselves heard are the shrill ones, devoid of thoughtfulness, nuance, and, often, logic.

This book is an antidote to all that.

I must admit that I approached it with some reluctance. A dual memoir? It was surely improbable, most likely impossible. But Scott Korb and Peter Bebergal are both very good writers on their own, and together they are even better. What might seem like a gimmick is in fact a magical conceit, a true dialogue between friends on a subject that dearly needs to be talked about.

It is all the more interesting because the two of them are traveling in different directions. Scott, coming from a super-religious background, is fighting to shed the strictures of his religion while remaining loyal to what he once hoped those strictures would help him attain. He longed then, and still longs, "to be powerful and unique," as do we all, and yet knows that humility is even more vital. Peter, after years of drug abuse and sundry other misbehaviors, is trying to build, brick by brick, a more prayerful life and a life that is also more meaningful. "But religious practice," he writes, "also happens outside the synagogue and the church. Religion binds people together by offering them a way to speak about their lives."

That is what this book is really about for both Peter and Scott: the meaning of meaning. Religion is merely a tool—granted, the main one, but still just a tool—that they are using to build a life of meaning.

Most religious memoirs inevitably circle back to the same irresistible, ineffable question: How real is God? But that is not the question that Scott and Peter wrestle with. Instead they address something that is, to my mind at least, far more interesting: How real is faith?

This book is their answer. In writing so honestly on the subject— the search for faith, its mysteries and glories and disappointments— they make it real. Their words on the page, born of ideas, become almost corporeal. And they don't even need to raise their voices to do so.

INTRODUCTION

— *Peter Bebergal and Scott Korb* —

THIS BOOK BEGAN with what has become, for many of us, a not-so-innocent and not-so-simple question: *Do you believe in God?*

We're nervous even to ask; simply posing the question reveals something about you, if only that you're earnest enough to care. And answering in either direction, yes or no, can often feel like a great risk, depending on the company you keep. This kind of exposure can be embarrassing. The question catches us with our, yes, Proverbial pants down. After all, "The simple believe everything, but the clever consider their steps." So for a good number of people these days, yes or no simply doesn't cover it. We step carefully around the question: Do you believe?

Well, we, longtime friends Peter Bebergal and Scott Korb, Jewish and Catholic, respectively, have something we've been dying to tell. We don't want to be embarrassed anymore. We're not mincing words. We're not ashamed. Yes, we believe. *But* . . .

To say that we believe means that at the center of our lives is an idea of God.

Now, our embarrassment, shame, nerves, and fear around making

1

THE FAITH BETWEEN US

this very simple claim have had mostly to do with wanting to keep
our faiths free of associations with scriptural literalism and religious narrow-mindedness. We haven't wanted to be misunder-
stood. And because we've been embarrassed and hesitant, our
professions of faith, when we've made them, have tended to be almost entirely defensive. Yes, we believe, but we're not like those
fundamentalists and the Bible-thumpers. Yes, we believe, but
we're not on the front lines arguing against gay marriage or stem-
cell research. Yes, we believe, but we're not praying to usher in the
end of the world. Yes, we believe, but we're not the Moral Majority. Yes, we believe, but we're not going to try to convince you to believe what we do.

All this backsliding, all these *buts*, have often made ours a negative faith. Because we find certain, frequently very public, religious
views not just distasteful but even culturally blinkered and politi-
cally dangerous—arguments for a six-thousand-year-old Earth, for
example, turn our stomachs as much as they offend the truths we
know about the natural world—until recently we'd turned inward.

Before we knew each other, our faiths had been our own private
affairs, pilgrimages we'd undertaken in the hope of both finding
and, yes, pleasing God. All alone, unfortunately we could do neither.

Faith is not, we've learned, a private matter at all. We're tired of
faith coming between us. God's will is that it may *live* between us.
Faith is nothing if not shared. And so, over the years, in becoming
faithful friends we've told each other stories about where we've
come from, how we've believed through our joys and our tragedies,
how we've faced God alone, how we've both sinned and overcome
sin, how we've both nearly died and overcome death. Some of those
stories follow in these pages. For us, this storytelling—religious
confession, in a way—has become a key to our religious lives. But
once we started talking, the important stories of our faith became

2

inseparable from the friendship itself. Not only were we finally opening up about faith, but we also began inspiring and teaching each other to live more faithfully. Most of the stories in this book exist only because there *is* a faith between us.

In the years before we met, our faith lives had become compartmentalized. We'd made our ways into and within communities that were at best skeptical, and at worst hostile, toward both religious sentiment and any appearance of belief in some religious truth. We understood why—again, hating literalism and religious sanctimony—and genuinely participated in that skepticism and hostility while at the same time privately praying and attending religious services. Often alone.

Although they did not start out this way, our approaches to religion had, by the time we met, become largely academic. As undergraduates, we took The Bible as Literature, looked for biblical allusions in literary texts, studied religion and politics, and distributed in creative-writing workshops stories and poems loaded with religious themes. Faith, or belief in God, was hardly a matter worth discussing. Skeptical of both the pious-seeming "College Catholics" and the overly studious and insular Hillel groups, back then we existed on the religious fringe, preferring rock shows and girls to Bible study and campus-sponsored Shabbat dinners. We each learned to pray quietly, and anxiously.

Later, though, we both studied theology in graduate school, and largely for the same reason: with the belief and hope that we could reconcile our academic interests, which included the desire for intellectual honesty and integrity, with our admittedly irrational religious devotion. What better places to do this, we thought, than divinity schools attached to major academic institutions?

Scott chose Union Theological Seminary in the City of New

York, which is affiliated with Columbia University and is the former home of neoorthodox theologian Reinhold Niebuhr and German theologian Dietrich Bonhoeffer, killed in 1945 for his part in an assassination plot against Hitler. Peter chose Harvard Divinity School, onetime home of American religious giants Ralph Waldo Emerson and George Santayana, and studied with Richard Niebuhr, son of the famous Union professor.

Entering Union at twenty-one, Scott was surrounded by believers, most of them ministers in training; starting in on second or third careers, many of his classmates were ten or twenty years older than he was. Carrying with him the skepticism he acquired in college (not to mention the cultural influences that shaped that skepticism, from indie rock music to literary journals), Scott was as interested in what New York had to teach him as he was in what he could learn in the classroom. Seminary became no less academic than college. He skipped chapel services, developed friendships with younger people outside the seminary, and began to find the historical Jesus more compelling than the one who worked miracles. Although still a devout Catholic who befriended the local priest and for a stretch went to Mass every day and taught catechism on the weekends, Scott left seminary with a flagging belief in the supernatural, no less alone in his faith than when he'd moved to the city, and with hardly any confidence at all in speaking about God.

At Harvard, Peter was surrounded by devout Catholics, staunch atheists, Wiccans, Episcopalians, just enough Jews for a minyan, and even a few ultraconservative Christians who loved going on archeological digs to the Middle East. And then there were the Unitarians, secularists, and postmodernists, the last of whom seemed to be in the majority and who eschewed religious language except when it was relativist and multicultural. God was nothing more than the "ground of being," if anything at all. When they weren't in class, Peter and his friends went to see independent films, read underground comics, slept with each other, and argued about postmodernism. On Friday nights, as local Jews made their way to services, Peter watched through the window of a German beer house while he and a group of classmates smoked cigars and ate chopped liver. Though embracing the secular theological culture, Peter also ached to be making his way with those Jews to synagogue. Yet he never would have said so. Even though he felt more at home with his friends, he still felt alone and longed for a connection with a religious community. In or out of the classroom, there was surprisingly little said about God.

We found each other after we left divinity school. Our meeting in the early part of 2001 was under fairly unremarkable circumstances. We both read and wrote for small, mostly online, literary magazines, most notable of which was the often imitated, archly ironic *McSweeney's*. We read online what the other person wrote, and before long started corresponding through e-mail addresses attached to the stories and letters we'd published. Nature then took its course. We became friends.

Of course, as we'd been with most of our other friends, we were quiet about our faith lives at first, as had become normal among people like us: in short, East Coast liberals with advanced degrees who read contemporary literature and listened to independent music. Relating our experiences of faith had never been easy. Having learned to protect ourselves from embarrassment in public, we rarely spoke explicitly about God, often throwing our hands up when asked to answer one way or another whether God existed or not. Palms turned up seemed a strange gesture for two men with graduate degrees in theology.

Yet fortunately, with each other, our language betrayed us. The tension between a comfortable and acceptable skepticism and our undeniable religious temperaments had created in us the hypersensitivity we needed to recognize each other as kindred spirits. Possessing something like what's known as "gaydar" in the queer community (but may be even queerer in our world), after a little hinting around Peter finally asked: *Do you believe in God?*

With each other we have finally learned to be more expressive about God. Over the same time we've grown more comfortable being expressive among other friends and family and, to some extent, in public. Through this effort, we've tried to prove that one can have an authentic religiosity and a genuine appreciation of holiness that is marked by healthy questioning and doubt—without needing to ever say anything definitively or universally about God.

Written by two people, this book contains a variety of ideas about God and a variety of approaches to talking about belief. We can't help it. One of us is Jewish. The other is Catholic. (And even within those categories we can often be inconsistent.) One of us has always been more mystical, often superstitious. The other has been more diligently disciplined, sometimes recklessly so—more pious in study and practice. And though not strictly bound to the rites and rituals of our old traditions, we remain deeply committed to engaging them in our religious practices. We do not live in perfect, unquestioning communion with our ancient laws and myths, but continually hear the collective echoes of those ancient, mythic voices. Our respective religious languages, interests, and sources—from the Bible to its commentaries, prayers, hymns, and jokes—infuse everything we want to say about God, and finally about all of God's creation, or the world. This was the great discovery of our friendship.

Yet as much as the language and myths of our traditions often highlight what is unique about our faiths—that God's covenant is marked by circumcision, say; or that, in Jesus, such laws no longer apply—we share another language as well, one of art and literature, music and sex, family and friendships, a cultural language that supports a much broader conception of faith. God can never be exhausted by traditionally religious language. Not only does no *one* tradition ever capture holiness, but from pop songs to birdsong, tics to tattoos, we find it everywhere.

Through our friendship—one based on curiosity, trust, and difference in matters of belief—we've come up with a moderate approach to faith, one that's easier to stomach both for us and, we've learned, for our communities than the louder, more extreme positions in the culture. We see myth as myth: edifying stories that tell only of the possibility of another world, and always in the service of this one. We see practice as practice, not only in our religious liturgies but more important, even, through our attentiveness and actions outside of worship, performing the will of God. Being friends takes practice. And we encourage each other to practice being better sons to our parents, lovers to our partners, and even fathers to our children. In the end, we see religion as a way to engage ethically with our commitments to God in daily life, rather than as a preparation for a final encounter with God in the afterlife. And all this without any shared belief in what God is or is not.

The faith between us is a faith in this world. Hastening the end of time, a key idea to many fundamentalist conceptions of religion, is to hasten the end of all we love. It is to hasten the end of practice. It is to do away with the languages we share, and represents a disastrous end of faith. Religious fundamentalism, like its opposite extreme, a vehemently secularist atheism, understands belief instrumentally and reads sacred texts literally. But to read scripture literally is to remove it from the world, to hide its frail yet boundlessly hopeful humanity behind some perfect, almighty hand of God. Lost are its literary beauty, its wonder, and the more complicated ethical and moral teachings developed over centuries by all religious traditions.

What follows are ten stories that aim to reveal how, through our friendship, we've come to have faith in God's creation. Placed side by side, alternating one after another, our individual stories are meant to interact, to carry on a conversation of faith like the ones we've had since that day we both admitted to believing in God. They draw on our entire lives of faith, from our first encounters with God to the ongoing struggles we still face together today, and explore our dealings with love, loss, drugs, sex, food, music—even our neuroses and neuralgias.

By now we've been telling each other these stories for years. And, as often happens with companions—spouses, twins, lifelong friends—we've developed the ability, and so that annoying habit, of finishing each other's sentences. Our alternating narratives, which make up the bulk of these pages, are the *stuff* of the faith lives we've shared with each other. At this point we could each tell the other's stories as if they were our own. And in many cases, especially as the stories reveal how our lives have converged and our faiths have grown together, moments from our narratives are even seen through a kind of shared vision. So in the spirit of our deepening companionship, we've attempted the literary equivalent of finishing each other's sentences: We've composed ten short epilogues to conclude each other's stories, in an experiment designed to show that while we don't always see eye to eye—and are often critical—our affinity in faith has bound us together to create that shared religious vision nonetheless.

Our hope is that in sharing this conversation, in appearing in public as faithful friends, we might also begin to hear other stories and participate in other conversations of belief, disbelief, hope, doubt, and the eternal desire to learn and do the will of God. We still long to find and please God. And we know we're better off trying to do this together.

THE TIC

— SK —

SLOWLY, TENSION BUILDS again over my right eye. And as usual when this happens—that is, constantly—I try to be patient. But after nearly thirty years, I know by now there's no way to wait it out. I never feel okay. I never really have.

My God! Where is he!

No matter how old I get, I can't help but feel like a little kid with my feet stretched out in front of me on a table, paper crinkling beneath me, sneakers pointing to the ceiling, fanning in and out. This exam room is so small. They should have left me out there with all the other sick people in the waiting room.

Where is the doctor?

Then, suddenly, my brow flashes under the pressure. And then my eye goes—*wink, wink!* I've prayed to God. I've pleaded with him. Yet this tic, a pull below the surface of my face, hasn't ever gone away. When the tension builds, the same muscles clench, slowly wind up in my head, and the pressure absolutely must find some release. So I make it happen, sometimes every few seconds. Over and over and over again. I can't help it.

I check myself in the mirror across the room, something I usually try to avoid in moments like this. I have to say, they're a little grotesque, all these little jerks in my face. I sometimes hate to look at myself.

I like to think this is no muscle spasm, that I give shape to each sudden expression on my face. But I've decided that I finally want a physician to see this. Dr. Gambarin keeps me waiting. His nurse passes through the hall again on her way to somewhere else. *Wait, I think, you have to see this. Look!* Then below my eye, I release the tension again through another quick but deep wink.

I slide my glasses back up the bridge of my nose, something I'm always having to do. For an actor friend of mine who does spot-on impressions, *this* is my quintessential gesture. In her mirror, I'm always readjusting my glasses or softly touching my face or massaging my jaw. Impressions of the tics themselves, I suppose, would be like doing a lazy eye or palsied wrist. Seems to me her motto is don't kick a man when he's down; and as long as she's known me, I guess I've always been down.

The nurse has already been in to take my pulse. It's normal. So is my blood pressure. I weigh the same as I did when I was twenty. I'm the same height. And when she left, I stretched my mouth open wide, behind her back.

That's better.

But it's always only better for a moment. That's when the tension moved up to my brow, after the nurse left, gradually building again around my eye as I waited for the doctor. Then there was the sudden dance on my forehead.

Even after all these years, doctors still make me nervous. And when I'm nervous my face goes even a little crazier. And to be honest, until recently I found a way to be pleased about this. Rather than ever seeing a doctor, both scared of what I might learn and assured I'd learn nothing at all, I'd done a little spiritual self-diagnosing. And as might be expected, I found myself to be in

throw off childish ways; we disapprove of the church's
doings; we appraise the church by its own standards and it
doesn't measure up; or we appraise ourselves and realize
we don't live up to what Christ and the church demand of us.

Mostly, though, we are ashamed because we lack the
resources of Catholic tradition that might enable us
to reconcile seeming opposites and make sense of the
absurdity we confront.

ays Elie, is a generation of young Catholics with "a seeming
nce, or inability to articulate our religious beliefs and act on
In me, this reluctance has also been due, at least in part, to
iness with the ostentation and defensiveness that in Amer-
gion mostly corresponds with literalism and evangelism,
ounds defiantly—against science, higher education, and
l elite"—from ten-thousand-member megachurches and
ve Christian radio. I've often been left with a question:
believing like a Christian fundamentalist, how do I ar-
ve of Christ without sounding like one?

many years since I've felt comfortable wearing my re-
 sleeve. (And I used to *love* my altar boy's robe.) For
h, through my tics it sufficed to wear it very plainly

nething of my early fear of God had lingered
owing religious doubt. Exactly what over time I'd
n and reject of traditional Catholic belief had al-
atter, though, when compared with a regular and
ion of a moral and religious life so intense it
bubble over. I'd come to know it as my *sufferings*.
is imagination, which has always taken the idea

perfect health. The tightness spreading uncontrollably through
my face had come to say something special about me. I was chosen
for this. By God. Or so I thought.

This appointment I'd made for January 12, 2006, was a standard
physical, something I hadn't been through in more than ten years.
At some point, after I'd built up the nerve, I'd ask Gambarin what
he thought about my face.

When I'd arrived about an hour earlier, I realized that little had
changed since I'd last seen a doctor. Clinics still make you wait
forever. As a new patient, I'd had some paperwork to fill out.
When the receptionist handed me a New York Methodist Hospital ID card, I noticed she'd messed up my birthday. "Excuse me,
ma'am," I'd said, leaning over the check-in counter and pointing
at the card. "I'm sorry. Something's wrong here. This should say
nineteen-seventy-six, not sixty-seven."

The woman took the card from me, glanced at it, and walked
away to make another one. She suggested that I have a seat.

Then it struck me: Could I really look thirty-eight? Had she
thought that could be right? 1967? Suddenly self-conscious of my
premature crow's-feet, I thought: Is that what these tics are doing
to me? Aging me?

When I was a child, these same facial tics accompanied long
staring jags over the breakfast table into the backyard, when the
leaves of our maple tree blurred in my sight as I thought about
God and heaven. Or about my dad, who had died at thirty-nine,
when I was only five.

A sickly child who suffered two bouts of pneumonia before my
fourth birthday, I also once needed an adrenaline shot to get my
heart going again. The staring fits had my mom convinced I had
epilepsy, or St. Paul's disease. But every test came back negative.

Even at five or six, I would have told her there was nothing to worry about. God knows I wasn't concerned about disease. On those mornings I was simply practicing being the very best starer I could be. And after those doctors' visits, as I continued staring out in the yard over the years, my mom mostly left me alone about what was obviously wrong with my face.

Even now, though, it must at times look to her as if I'm choking to death. Following those regular occasions when my mouth goes inexplicably wide, my mother has often wondered whether I'm having trouble breathing. *No, no, Mom, I'm just fine*, I've always said. Then I've changed the subject. And she's seemed happy to oblige.

For most of my life, though, she's been the only one to say anything at all. And I've been happy to oblige all the other people who have nothing to say, because by and large the tugs in my face have always been an embarrassment. They're a weakness. An imperfection. A flaw in my makeup. As much as possible, I've waited until I'm out of sight before opening this gaping mouth, or sometimes, if I can make it seem normal, I'll incorporate a facial tic into a laugh. I'll turn away from conversation. I'll cup my face with my hand and lean in to listen more closely.

But, of course, people have always noticed. As much as I've hoped to be fooling everyone, I never have. Like the friend who refuses to highlight the tics in her performances of me, other people have ignored it as well. They've played along.

I've never talked about what might be wrong with me. I had no idea. And deep down I actually feared it. So by now I'd gone ten years without seeing a doctor. Looking around, I knew this giant room was filled with sick people, or potentially sick people, all waiting. I was one of the potentially sick people. I always had been.

Dr. Gambarin had come off a long list provi insurance company. *His office is close. Speaks En internal medicine.* I'd decided he'd be fine. Two making hasty choices after letting my insuran no intention of ever seeing him anyway. But changed. I'd grown curious, even concerne

What is wrong with me?

I've always been a person of faith. As steeped in Bible stories, I was possesse lieved in the absolute reality of heave days, we sang church songs in the f Mass. Not believing never crossed everyone I knew seemed to know

In recent years, though, like broadly speaking, "young" Catl has been easy. As with many of us who doubt at least as much as much from our traditions mention of God, much less quiet. These days, finding and great swaths of an harsh, and unyielding (if many young Catholics, low Catholic writer P

[A]mong the ch been supplant about our ch are ashame ashamed:

16

throw off childish ways; we disapprove of the church's
doings; we appraise the church by its own standards and it
doesn't measure up; or we appraise ourselves and realize
we don't live up to what Christ and the church demand of us.

Mostly, though, we are ashamed because we lack the
resources of Catholic tradition that might enable us
to reconcile seeming opposites and make sense of the
absurdity we confront.

Ours, says Elie, is a generation of young Catholics with "a seeming
reluctance, or inability to articulate our religious beliefs and act on
them." In me, this reluctance has also been due, at least in part, to
an uneasiness with the ostentation and defensiveness that in American
religion mostly corresponds with literalism and evangelism,
and that sounds defiantly—against science, higher education, and
the "liberal elite"—from ten-thousand-member megachurches and
conservative Christian radio. I've often been left with a question:
While not believing like a Christian fundamentalist, how do I articulate
a love of Christ without sounding like one?

It's been many years since I've felt comfortable wearing my religion
on my sleeve. (And I used to *love* my altar boy's robe.) For
a time, though, through my tics it sufficed to wear it very plainly
on my face.

Indeed, something of my early fear of God had lingered
through my growing religious doubt. Exactly what over time I'd
come to question and reject of traditional Catholic belief had almost
ceased to matter, though, when compared with a regular and
endless articulation of a moral and religious life so intense it
couldn't help but bubble over. I'd come to know it as my *sufferings*.

To my religious imagination, which has always taken the idea

Dr. Gambarin had come off a long list provided by my health insurance company. *His office is close. Speaks English. Specializes in internal medicine.* I'd decided he'd be fine. Two years earlier, while making hasty choices after letting my insurance lapse, I really had no intention of ever seeing him anyway. But since then things had changed. I'd grown curious, even concerned.

What is wrong with me?

I've always been a person of faith. As a devoted and pious child, steeped in Bible stories, I was possessed by a fear of God and believed in the absolute reality of heaven, hell, and purgatory. Sundays, we sang church songs in the family car—both to and from Mass. Not believing never crossed my mind. And I wasn't alone; everyone I knew seemed to know God.

In recent years, though, like a good number of modern and, broadly speaking, "young" Catholics, I can't say that my faith life has been easy. As with many of my generation's faithful—those of us who doubt at least as much as we ever believe, and reject at least as much from our traditions as we ever embrace—for me the mere mention of God, much less Jesus, has often been cause for real disquiet. These days, finding much of Christian orthodoxy absurd and great swaths of ancient Catholic dogma barren—lifeless, harsh, and unyielding (if also just simply too vast to cover)—I, like many young Catholics, can be nothing but uneasy in my faith. Fellow Catholic writer Paul Elie describes the experience well:

> [A]mong the church's younger members, Catholic guilt has been supplanted by Catholic *shame*—a deep embarrassment about our church and its presence in the culture. In part we are ashamed for the reasons Christians have always felt ashamed: we associate faith with childhood and are eager to

Even at five or six, I would have told her there was nothing to worry about. God knows I wasn't concerned about disease. On those mornings I was simply practicing being the very best starer I could be. And after those doctors' visits, as I continued staring out in the yard over the years, my mom mostly left me alone about what was obviously wrong with my face.

Even now, though, it must at times look to her as if I'm choking to death. Following those regular occasions when my mouth goes inexplicably wide, my mother has often wondered whether I'm having trouble breathing. *No, no, Mom, I'm just fine*, I've always said. Then I've changed the subject. And she's seemed happy to oblige.

For most of my life, though, she's been the only one to say anything at all. And I've been happy to oblige all the other people who have nothing to say, because by and large the tugs in my face have always been an embarrassment. They're a weakness. An imperfection. A flaw in my makeup. As much as possible, I've waited until I'm out of sight before opening this gaping mouth, or sometimes, if I can make it seem normal, I'll incorporate a facial tic into a laugh. I'll turn away from conversation. I'll cup my face with my hand and lean in to listen more closely.

But, of course, people have always noticed. As much as I've hoped to be fooling everyone, I never have. Like the friend who refuses to highlight the tics in her performances of me, other people have ignored it as well. They've played along.

I've never talked about what might be wrong with me. I had no idea. And deep down I actually feared it. So by now I'd gone ten years without seeing a doctor. Looking around, I knew this giant room was filled with sick people, or potentially sick people, all waiting. I was one of the potentially sick people. I always had been.

perfect health. The tightness spreading uncontrollably through my face had come to say something special about me. I was chosen for this. By God. Or so I thought.

This appointment I'd made for January 12, 2006, was a standard physical, something I hadn't been through in more than ten years. At some point, after I'd built up the nerve, I'd ask Gambarin what he thought about my face.

When I'd arrived about an hour earlier, I realized that little had changed since I'd last seen a doctor. Clinics still make you wait forever. As a new patient, I'd had some paperwork to fill out. When the receptionist handed me a New York Methodist Hospital ID card, I noticed she'd messed up my birthday. "Excuse me, ma'am," I'd said, leaning over the check-in counter and pointing at the card. "I'm sorry. Something's wrong here. This should say nineteen-seventy-six, not sixty-seven."

The woman took the card from me, glanced at it, and walked away to make another one. She suggested that I have a seat.

Then it struck me: Could I really look thirty-eight? Had she thought that could be right? 1967? Suddenly self-conscious of my premature crow's-feet, I thought: Is that what these tics are doing to me? Aging me?

When I was a child, these same facial tics accompanied long staring jags over the breakfast table into the backyard, when the leaves of our maple tree blurred in my sight as I thought about God and heaven. Or about my dad, who had died at thirty-nine, when I was only five.

A sickly child who suffered two bouts of pneumonia before my fourth birthday, I also once needed an adrenaline shot to get my heart going again. The staring fits had my mom convinced I had epilepsy, or St. Paul's disease. But every test came back negative.

of chosenness more seriously than anything else, I was in good shape. Strange physical defects have always meant something special to God. As sufferings go, I could not have had better company. From the Old Testament I had Moses, and from the New Testament, the mighty St. Paul.

Moses is famous for his stammer. And when called by God from within the burning bush to deliver the Israelites from slavery, Moses can hardly believe it: "O my Lord, I have never been eloquent, neither in the past nor even now that you have spoken to your servant; but I am slow of speech and slow of tongue." But the Lord persists: "Who gives speech to mortals? Who makes them mute or deaf, seeing or blind? Is it not I, the Lord? Now go, and I will be with your mouth and teach you what you are to speak." Continuing to complain, Moses suggests that the Lord choose someone else and God gets angry. But quickly relenting—this is a God you can argue with—he agrees to be with Moses' brother Aaron, too: "[Aaron] indeed shall speak for you to the people; he shall serve as a mouth for you."

The stammer, though, becomes a sign of Moses' even greater exceptionality. Not just a prophet of God (a lesser role that gets passed on to Aaron), at the moment he responds to God's own stammering call—"Moses! Moses!"—he assumes a far greater function: "You shall serve as God for [Aaron]." An uneasy Moses becomes the very *source* of divine teachings, and largely because of his imperfect speech, his involuntary pauses and repetitions.

Less well known, perhaps, although in obvious ways more relevant to my Christian imagination, is the case of St. Paul. According to his letters, Paul, the apostle to the Gentiles whose writing and ideas dominate the New Testament, had a "physical infirmity" that many historians and biblical scholars agree was probably epilepsy. By their account, the first evidence of this neurological disorder appears when Paul, then known as Saul, suffers a seizure and is thrown to the ground.

Recounted in the Acts of the Apostles, this becomes the most significant moment of his life. Until this time a severe persecutor of Christians, Saul, "still breathing threats and murder against the disciples of the Lord," is visited by Jesus on his way to round up and imprison the early Christian community in Damascus, some sixty miles northeast of the Sea of Galilee. Suddenly, as he approaches the city, a flash of light from heaven—unapparent to his traveling companions—knocks Saul down, and he hears a voice say, "Saul, Saul, why do you persecute me?" This miraculous visitation, occurring after Jesus had already ascended into heaven, shocks and confuses Saul, leaving him temporarily blinded. Led into Damascus, Saul recovers there, and after three days is greeted by a Christian disciple named Ananias. Laying his hands on Saul, Ananias announces that Jesus had appeared to him as well, sending him to Saul so that Saul might regain his sight and be filled with the Holy Spirit. The biblical scene ends famously: "And immediately something like scales fell from his eyes, and his sight was restored. Then he got up and was baptized, and after taking some food, he regained his strength." Saul soon becomes known as Paul.

Over and over throughout scripture—say, from Abraham's covenant with God, marked by circumcision, to Jacob's wrestling bout with an angel—we find similarly miraculous visions and often violent interactions with the Almighty, not to mention a good number of name changes: Abraham was first called Abram; Jacob becomes known as Israel. These are the sorts of things we expect from our holy books. After all, chronicling and making meaning of man's encounters with God is, more or less, the very point of myth. But Paul's encounter is different.

And were it not for a few strange and telling moments in his own writing—the story from Acts is not a self-report—we might find nothing at all unusual in the conversion of Christianity's greatest early evangelist.

Paul begins his public ministry after the vision. Sending letters to fledgling communities from Galatia in Asia Minor, throughout Greece, and into Europe with the hope of unifying and building up the early church, Paul offers himself as a model while admonishing his followers against arrogance. "And you are puffed up!" he complains to the Corinthians. "I appeal to you, then," he writes, "be imitators of me." "Friends," he writes to the Galatians, "I beg you, become as I am, for I also have become as you are." To a degree that the Acts of the Apostles never describes, though, Paul, in his own writings, often seems not merely humbled but humiliated by his conversion. His very ministry, he writes, originated in an unsettling—both for him and his followers—physical defect. "You know that it was because of a physical infirmity that I first announced the gospel to you."

In Paul's story, we see again that God chooses, in unexpected ways, the ones we'd least expect: the frightened and unsure, the imperfect and self-conscious. In other words, a physical imperfection beyond one's control—say, a facial tic—could very well be the mark of God.

Either that, of course, or maybe it's Satan at work.

Despite the good it seemed to do him, whatever the actual nature of Paul's condition, he did not always possess Moses' confidence that it was a gracious God who had marked him. Whatever it was that seized and threw him to the ground—whether Jesus or some dysfunctional brain tissue—in the moment of this new religious calling, Paul is rebuked. He is toppled and shamed. Later, in a second letter to the church of Corinth, perhaps still prone to the

THE FAITH BETWEEN US

arrogance he demonstrated while persecuting Christians, Paul again offers his own life as the model. He writes:

> To keep me from being too elated, a thorn was given to me in the flesh, a messenger of Satan to torment me, to keep me from being too elated. Three times I appealed to the Lord about this, that it would leave me, but he said to me, "My grace is sufficient for you, for power is made perfect in weakness." So, I will boast all the more gladly of my weaknesses, so that the power of Christ may dwell in me. Therefore I am content with weaknesses, insults, hardships, persecutions, and calamities for the sake of Christ; for whenever I am weak, then I am strong.

A thorn in his flesh, Paul's physical sufferings tormented him. From the moment of his conversion, he was made weak for the sake of the service of Christ. Appeals to God go unanswered; he's left with a typically Christian riddle about weakness being the most perfect power. Paul suffered the pain of holiness. And yet somehow at the center of his life is Satan, poking around inside his head with a pitchfork.

In the year before I found my way to Gambarin's office, my own sufferings—which, it should be said, are probably as severe as a stammer but nothing at all compared with epileptic seizures—had reached the height of their religious significance.

Believing myself both chosen by God and tormented by Satan, I lived somewhere between Moses and St. Paul. And so, when faced with a moral problem—jealousy or envy, impatience, lust, a lie—I believed my sufferings got worse. More fierce. Deeper. More regular. More visible. My face took my moral temperature. But like Paul, I saw myself become more perfect by my imperfections, at one point unable even to admit that these constant reminders to be good in the world didn't in fact make me totally without flaws. To my mind, I became not just your everyday freak but something of a literary character, one of Flannery O'Connor's prophet freaks, a grotesque figure who, it's been said, "startles the unwitting reader to attention." Aware that I was no longer hiding it, my face instead proudly said, "Look at me!"

Pride is at once among the seven deadliest sins and a common and celebrated religious impulse. From a Christian perspective, according to the Gospel of Mark, pride is a defilement that comes from within, ranking up there with murder, lying, blasphemy, and just being a fool. Yet also typical among religious types, despite its acknowledged sinfulness, is the kind of pride we're born with, baptized into, or circumcised for, the knowledge that God made us exceptional, special, and chosen. It should come as no surprise that I had grown to be quietly proud of myself and my *sufferings*.

And as much as people might have been startled now by the angel-devil showdown happening all over my face, and as much as I believed in its potential to be instructive, short of developing a tic of their own, nobody could compete. And as much as it now pains me to acknowledge it, nobody in his right mind wanted a tic.

It was as if God had said to me: *Your power is made perfect in weakness*. For all the gains I believed I was making in developing a faith rooted in the worldliness and voluntary weaknesses necessary for charity and compassion, I still somewhere longed to be powerful and unique, which would make me, as always, alone.

This has always been the threat of faith.

Because faith can often feel like this, an involuntary and embarrassing tug, an annoyance even, something that rises from just below the surface. It can feel as if you're born with it. Where we go wrong—where I've *always* gone wrong—is in letting the tug alone make us feel chosen.

Because I've learned that as much as faith may seem innate, at the same time we're also completely responsible for it. This lesson went untaught in the small-town church of my childhood, where God—and short of him, his priest—controlled everything, and where I first developed the belief that discipline, and any related suffering, was the saintliest virtue. Our rituals, from Holy Mass to the practice of the sacraments, were designed by God, our prayers composed by him. Pleasing God meant following his commandments. Faith itself was a gift from God that you gave back simply by believing in him absolutely and acting accordingly.

But now I believe that where faith is concerned, you control its shape, the form it takes in your life, all of the strange and disfiguring symptoms that emerge. From the wonder inspired by stories of miraculous healings to the compassion that wells up at the sight of a beggar to the awe that overwhelms you in moments of lovemaking, you sense, *God is here, again.* And you do something more than just believe. Belief itself is not enough. You mark the appearance as bigger than you. You pray. You give. You surrender.

Because while it's true you can always control the ritual or act—the practice of faith—I've found that when God shows up, constantly yet always somewhat unexpectedly, you can't *not* do something about it.

And over time you really start to love it. The hope is that you learn to articulate and act on your beliefs. You become proud of how this divine tug appears in your life, and stop being embarrassed at the names you have to give it: love, faith, hope, even *Jesus.*

None of these names may be accurate. They all may simply be figures of speech. But with faith, what else is there? You feel something—it pulls—and you cannot help but call it something, try to say something meaningful about it. Call it the love of Christ, the will of God: It doesn't matter, really.

What matters is how the meaning you've made of faith moves you, and that you take responsibility to act on it.

Gambarin is a huge Russian, and when he finally arrives, the exam begins immediately. He moves fast. As the doctor checks my abdomen, pressing into my side with good humor, he's not expecting to find anything wrong. I'm in fine shape.

"Does this hurt?"

"No, no," I say a little impatiently. We run through a series of questions and answers about habits and vices: no drugs, the occasional half-cigarette that I always regret, a good amount of social drinking. The little sex I've had has been safe. I'm careful about what I eat. He laughs at me when I tell him that I was, until recently, a vegan.

The doctor is breathing heavy and sweating a little above his lip. He seems even more enormous now than when he entered the room. *What am I doing here?*

I'm reminded when I feel my face starting to tug again, and so begin to explain the problem. There are visuals. "It looks like this," I say, as I wink suddenly at him.

Bemused, he doesn't bat an eye. "That's all?" he says.

"No. This too." I demonstrate the sick yawn. "And this," I say as I raise my eyebrows.

He rolls his eyes and presses into my side again. "How about this? Does this hurt?"

"No, nothing hurts. But what do you think about my face?"

He's not impressed. "This is the only thing that's ever been wrong with you? These . . . tics. It's nothing at all."

While not fatal, the most typical facial neuralgia, known as *tic douloureux* and sometimes the "suicide disease," is commonly described as the worst pain known to man. It is sharp and stabbing. American pragmatist philosopher Charles Sanders Peirce, who believed, among other things, that God's love had shaped evolution, and that there is ultimate meaning in the universe, suffered from it, and turned to opium, morphine, and cocaine to cope. Just before his death—while he was also suffering from cancer—Peirce claimed that writing was all he could do to relieve his pain.

Thank God my neuralgia is atypical. To call the sensations painful would be inaccurate. The trigeminal nerve, Gambarin explained, resides deep in my skull; its root enters the brain stem. My tics follow the paths of the nerve's three branches, which allow for sensations of touch, pain, and temperature for my forehead and eye, throughout my cheek, and into my lower face and jaw. The nerve also allows me to chew.

Gambarin said there's no telling why the nerve is damaged. But it's unlikely that God has anything to do with it. Medically, there is really nothing to be done. If it were affecting only one of the three branches, perhaps he could treat it. With neither an apparent cause nor an effective cure, though, I'll just continue on. This isn't at all disappointing. As I've said, while I never feel quite right—which makes me assume that no one ever really does—the tics don't actually hurt. And after thirty years, if it's true they're not going to kill me, I can't think of any reason to try to stop them—especially now that they don't make me feel so special. I've never been chosen. But, of course, I didn't see the doctor for a cure, necessarily, just a diagnosis that wasn't so spiritual, the same one that anyone with my condition would get. I visited Gambarin's office because I'm through pursuing personal salvation.

In recent years, I've experienced a kind of ongoing religious conversion. Still Christian, I no longer hope to be saved. Still Catholic, I no longer strive toward sainthood. A convert of a kind, I've taken to heart the words of a friend, an actual convert to Judaism from a Catholicism that, for all its "trafficking in the idea of perfection," looked a great deal like mine: "As a Jew, I would never become a saint, a tzaddik," he's written. "But I could achieve the supreme distinction of becoming a mensch—a man."

For me, this is the new measure of faith. God does not call us to become like angels in heaven—"God has plenty of angels," as one ancient rabbi has said—but to live as his creatures on Earth, which means together, according to his will.

So faith is never best articulated in terms that puff us up and set us apart. (It's possible that actual faith can never be articulated this way.) To me, St. Paul seems wiser now than ever to preach against such arrogance. Building up his early church, he called its members the body of Christ, which is still the central Christian metaphor. (We *eat* the body of Christ; we *are* the body of Christ.) In his letters, Paul admits no distinction between Jew or Greek, slave or free, woman or man: "Now you are the body of Christ and individually members of it."

> But God has so arranged the body, giving the greater honor
> to the inferior member, that there may be no dissension
> within the body, but the members may have the same care
> for one another. If one member suffers, all suffer together
> with it; if one member is honored, all rejoice together
> with it.

I like to think of myself as an unruly cowlick on the body of Christ.

I called Peter from outside Gambarin's office. "I have an untreatable neurological disorder," I announced. "Trigeminal neuralgia . . . T-R-I-G-E-M-I-N-A-L."

He immediately went hunting on the Internet.

Now that I've begun talking about it—now that I'm less embarrassed and scared—most of my family and friends know what's wrong with my face. My mother has explained that she'd always just assumed it was harmless. She and I shared the logic: *If it hasn't killed you yet* . . . Another friend figured I occasionally used cocaine. Though I don't believe them, certain friends denied ever noticing anything at all. And although we've had more than one conversation about it, my impressionist friend still hasn't incorporated these most distinctive gestures into her act. Perhaps she'll slip someday and perform my winks.

From my own research, I've learned that it may get worse in time, that my atypical facial neuralgia may become more like the typical kind, *tic douloureux*, the suicide disease. And knowing this exposes me a little still, spiritually. As with any conversion, mine has left a little residue of the former faith.

A friend recently asked, "Do you wish you had the suicide disease?"

"No way," I answered. "I've seen severe pain and severe pain is no good."

But she knows me well enough to ask. And to ask again (which she has). My yearning for sainthood, which began as a child and intensified from there, has always made me assume that suffering is better than pleasure, and that personal discipline is the only way of God. So far I've made a life of it. It's possible there may be no clean conversion.

"Are you secretly excited for the pain?" she continued.

I had to think about it. Typical though it may be, the Worst Pain Known To Man would set me apart. That sort of faith still pulls. But I'm learning better. We suffer together. We rejoice together. We believe together. There may be no faith but the faith between us. And like any of us, it's not perfect.

So:

"No," I answered, a little unsure of myself. "I'm not secretly excited for the pain."

EPILOGUE
— *PB* —

As with Scott, my faith is not discernable by appearance alone. And while I've never had a tic to serve as an external sign of my religious struggles, I have something like it. I don't drink, and in the social circles that I inhabit, people wonder about it in much the same way. They have opinions and ideas, but most people don't ask. They just know, since I tell people fairly quickly that I don't drink. Sometimes this makes for awkward moments, like having to pass on the rum-soaked cake, or asking that they please not douse the barbecue sauce with whiskey when everyone else at the dinner party was looking forward to it. In many ways it separates me, makes me special, sets me apart.

There has long been controversy over the biblical idea that Jews are God's chosen people. Some have used this to charge Jews with the sins of pride and greed. And I'm sure many Jews hear in the infamous Exodus verse a calling that they are special, that our spiritual condition places us above others:

> Now therefore, if you obey my voice and keep my
> covenant, you shall be my treasured possession out of
> all the people. Indeed, the whole Earth is mine, but you
> shall be for a priestly kingdom and a holy people.

But there is another way to understand the idea of a holy, or perhaps priestly, people, where being chosen for this role is not one of degree but one of responsibility. As Jews, we are charged with living as an example, and more than that, charged with being of service. My sobriety functions in much the same way, to serve as an example to others who struggle, to be of service to those who might need help. And in this way Scott is chosen also. His belief, one of deep regard for human beings and for the world we call home, *is* special. His is a unique Christianity, and so he has a responsibility to be an example to others of how to love, and to serve those who need help.

While it was somewhat different when we first met, I learned of Scott's faith in an exchange over e-mail. I had only actually met him once before in person—both of us were attending a reading in Boston. And for the next year we corresponded daily. Slowly, details began to emerge. We'd both studied theology in graduate school. One Sunday Scott wrote that he had just returned from Mass. He taught religious education. In another note I wrote that I was going to temple on Yom Kippur. Our references and allusions were curious: the Bible, Flannery O'Connor, Martin Buber, and Dietrich Bonhoeffer. Our religious lives seemed more than tradition, more than just familial habits. There seemed to be something at stake. Then one day, while my son played on the floor at my feet, I asked Scott if he believed in God. Not only did he answer yes, but he also seemed to know exactly what I meant by the question.

The few other times I had openly admitted to someone that my faith was more than agnosticism, conversation usually turned to the meaning of the words I used. Do I believe God is a person? Do I think God has a body? Is there a heaven? A hell? I tried to avoid having to answer these kinds of questions because I was afraid anything I said about God would be taken literally, no matter how much I tried to argue that I didn't mean any of it that way. In certain company I might not talk about religion at all. A number of close friends are openly hostile to any idea of not only organized religion, but any kind of spiritual worldview. Sometimes, when I am staying over at a friend's house, or even my in-laws', I find it impossible to say, "Excuse me for a while, I have to say my prayers." I can think of nothing more embarrassing. So I find a time, often when everyone else has gone to bed, and I sit on the floor in the dark and pray.

Scott knew when I asked if he believed that I was asking if he had doubt also. I was not asking if he was in perfect communion with a higher power, not asking if he was "born again," not even asking if he believed God appeared to Moses on Mount Sinai. I was asking if he looked for the sacred in his life, if he had encountered holiness. And then when I confirmed that I believed too, we didn't speak explicitly about faith for a long time after. It was as if believing in God was simply a state of being like our age, where we were born, the names of our parents. Our faith wasn't something to talk about. For perhaps the first time in either of our lives, it became simply a way to talk to each other. It was colloquial. It was slang.

Many of my friends might still peg me as agnostic. More comfortable than ever admitting a belief in God, I still rarely let on that I am deeply theistic, that I pray, or that when I fast on Yom Kippur I am seeking real atonement. There is no risk in saying, "Well, there might be something, but I'm not sure what it is." No one faults anyone's agnosticism. And for those people I know whose belief does lean toward some kind of theism, they have no religious life to speak of. It's easy to stand between worlds, with no challenge, with no religious practice. As a Jew, this is made all the more effortless. If, say, at a party someone wants to know about my religion, I might simply say that I'm Jewish, but that says nothing about my conception of God, or if I even have one. Luckily, Jews get a kind of get-out-of-jail-free card in regards to public religiousness. There is a certain presumption that Jewish practice is merely tradition, that reading out of the Haggadah on Passover is like hunting for Easter eggs on Easter. If I tell someone I am going to synagogue on Rosh Hashanah, there is no hidden wonderment about my belief. Of course Jews go to synagogue on holidays. Religious practice doesn't imply a belief in God. Belief in God is irrelevant.

Ironically, the irrelevance of belief is a very Jewish idea. The first commandment reads, "You shall love the Lord your God with all your heart." There is nothing here about belief. Belief is either presupposed or else the reality of God is so certain that having "faith" in something you cannot have a direct sensory experience with is redundant. In this sense, Judaism is not concerned with faith.

More important, simply believing in God alone does not serve the world in any way. While plenty of the Jewish commandments are about religious ritual and dietary restrictions, many more are about how to live in this world ethically, how to be honest in matters both personal and public, how to be charitable, how to be just. Neither God, human beings, nor the world are improved by faith alone. It seems counterintuitive because there is a natural religious tendency to want to believe that faith alone makes us inherently good. (In the same way we often think that enough remorse should redeem us without our having to pay consequences.) But neither the first commandment, nor any of the following, mention faith at all. The first commandment is interested in love. Even the Hebrew word for faith—*amunah*—makes this relationship clear. The word for faith (or belief) is a derivation of the word *amen*, which is a declaration of an oath, a promise. In this sense, faith is not about believing that God exists, but rather believing that in some way we can be in relation with God, that we can each trust the other to fulfill the terms of this oath—in much the same way that we must relate to a loved one or a friend. In a way, we enter into an agreement of sorts, a contract that we will act faithfully, we will return phone calls, pick up the check now and again, remember birthdays.

Ultimately it doesn't matter whether or not God exists in some provable or literal way, but rather that I believe in God. And I trust that God believes in me.

Around the same time that Scott and I told each other we believed, I told Scott that I didn't drink, and not only that, but the circumstances that led to my sobriety. Not many people get those details, but since I had seen his tic without his wanting me to, Scott had to see mine as well. And in much the same way that Scott has come to understand that his tic is not a spiritual affliction, something that marks him as chosen, I have to work so that my sobriety doesn't make me feel unique. And yet, sobriety *is* a spiritual condition. What led me to it *was* a spiritual affliction. But rather than make me unique, it makes me humble.

Being a priestly person, as Scott still fancies himself to one degree or another, takes a great deal of discipline. It's a condition of action, of active participation in our relationships, in our work, and in our communities. And as with my sobriety, it means constant vigilance. Much like Scott, I used to think the opposite was true, that to be special meant to be handpicked by God. And if this was true, then my very being in the world was enough to be faithful. I saw belief as passive, silent, and private. Gradually, though, I've come to understand that faith is exactly as Scott has been teaching me. Faith may be less about what you believe and much, much more about what you do. Like art, inspiration can take you only so far. The real expression of an idea arises out of craft. Picasso's abstract work can be understood only within the context of his whole technique. Hidden in the thin and oblique lines that form the figure of a bull is a formal ability that took years of work. Faith alone brings us no closer to any ideal. It's the willingness to be a person who acts faithfully that leads us to a religious life. Faith takes practice.

THE CLARINET

I WAS SITTING in an extremely hot third-floor apartment in the summer of 1999 with a clarinet balanced precariously between my fingers. The teacher had just shown me how to wet the reed with my saliva and secure it to the mouthpiece with the ligature. Sweat from my forehead dripped down into my eyes. My neck and shirt were soaked. I was trembling. I started to have second thoughts: This is crazy. I was thirty-two years old, I had never played an instrument in my life, and here I was on a summer day with an instrument that one associates with the school band. I wagered that everyone else in the whole city was outside playing sports. But I placed the mouthpiece to my lips and, following my teacher's directions, blew some air into the instrument.

It made a sound.

It sounded like a clarinet.

With that sound, I began to lose some of my uncertainty about what I was taking on here. I learned how to take the clarinet apart, clean it, and how to put it back together. I learned which fingers are assigned to which keys. I played "Twinkle, Twinkle, Little Star" at my first lesson. It wasn't Artie Shaw, but it sounded like I pulled it down from heaven. It sounded a little like my faith: uncertain, tremulous, earnest, and a little squawky. But also, as with my faith, in taking up this instrument I was deciding to make the leap into the unknown because, while I didn't exactly know what was on the other side, I could hear its echo from across the abyss. It sounded like a song I had been carrying in my head my whole life. My family descends from Eastern European Jews, and while no one in my immediate family played the clarinet, I could hear the sound of tradition, of community and exile, of faith itself, in the warbly exhale of my own playing. I hoped in the chambers of the clarinet I would learn how to love God. Maybe even love God like a Jew.

Even as a child I listened to music believing that somewhere there was the song that could explain everything, that carried the secrets of the universe in its rhythms. Back then, I sought God in a similar way, believing in a perfect idea I could form, a perfect experience I could have that would undeniably reveal God's existence. But this was a private faith, one part inspiration and one part a sense of, or desire for, my chosenness. If I was the right kind of person and thought the right thoughts, I would be given access to some hidden wisdom. I looked for this wisdom everywhere. It might be hidden in the subtext of J.R.R. Tolkien's *Lord of the Rings* trilogy. It might be found in my friend's parents' dirty magazines. At night I lay in bed, for hours fantasizing about superheroes and magic powers. And I wished every night for God to give me a sign that he was real. But mostly I thought the truth might be in music.

All I really had access to at first was the sugary pop of the seventies and a Fantastic Four comic book record I played on a plastic record player that opened like a suitcase. But from my older brother Eric's room I heard music that was stirring; tracks from the Beatles' *White Album*, Cat Stevens singing "Trouble." Sometimes I would sit in Eric's room and he would purposely play me the creepiest and most disturbing songs: the Beatles' "Revolution #9"; "Uncle Ernie" and "Acid Queen" by the Who. This world was like the Secret Society of Super Villains, an underground network of delinquents and miscreants, but instead of crime they traded in rich and complicated emotions: sexual, aggressive, and religious. The spiritual longing in Eric's rock 'n' roll was palpable. I became attuned to it. I was desperately looking for it. And so when I was twelve, I entered into the proud tradition of little brothers everywhere—without his permission, I started listening to my older brother's records.

Like a thief, I stole into Eric's room and quietly, secretly, played his albums. Lying on Eric's floor, his massive headphones hugging my head, I discovered the excess of rock 'n' roll. I raced through Eric's collection, learning quickly what was worth repeated listenings—the Beatles, David Bowie, Queen, Iggy Pop, Pink Floyd. These were the prayers of a culture: a liturgy of sex, Eastern spirituality, blues, folk, raga, psychedelia, and drugs. It was with a strange mix of eagerness and terror that I would willingly listen to the Who's *Tommy*.

Certain album covers made me so uneasy that I wouldn't even play the records: Led Zeppelin's *Houses of the Holy* and the Rolling Stones' *Sticky Fingers* (yes, it had the working zipper). But I would look at them over and over again, letting the anxiety well up in me until I couldn't take it anymore. I was looking for something I had no name for yet, but whatever it was called, it was throbbing in the speakers and in my groin.

We have lost something with the advent of the CD and even more so with the mp3. There is no more sitting on the floor with an album in your lap. The whole thing was tactile and edgy. In Eric's room, I had my hands all over the music and the musicians. For the next year I traced the outline of Bowie's hips and Chrissie

Hynde's lips as she yelled, "Fuck off!" on the song "Precious" while my Legos sat on the other side of the wall. All the order of my world collapsed in wave after wave of my brother's records.

From then on I chased music as a transformative experience. Gradually I understood that I was looking for an ultimate truth, what the theologian Paul Tillich calls one's "ultimate concern." I would keep looking for it in music, and then later in sex and other more illicit and ultimately futile means. It would be some time before the truth I was after would reveal itself in an unexpected way.

My clarinet is not a very good one, but it only cost me about seventy-five dollars. The woman who sold it to me told me it had belonged to her son when he was taking lessons in grade school. I gathered he didn't do much with it after that. It might have made more sense for me to have chosen a guitar. The guitar was the principal instrument of the bands I listened to in Eric's room. It was the feedback of a guitar still vibrating in my heart that brought me here in the first place. I can identify easily with its sound, something so familiar, so engrained in my consciousness. But as much as the guitar defines the sound of the music I love and know intimately, it was the clarinet that actually lured me as if with a siren call. Never before, in over thirty years obsessed with music, had I had the desire to actually play an instrument. Until the clarinet.

What initially drew me to the clarinet was the work of David Krakauer, a clarinetist who has worked with the avant-garde composer John Zorn and was a member of the illustrious klezmer band the Klezmatics. Prior to hearing Krakauer, the clarinet had always seemed unremarkable, except maybe in the glissando of the opening strains of Gershwin's "Rhapsody in Blue." But Krakauer was trying to combine two seemingly disparate things. This tension between tradition and experimentation, between the tether of the past and the pull of the future, has always figured deeply in my religious life. And here was a sound—not a theology but a sound—that not only bridged the two but retained the tension. Krakauer's music is challenging precisely because he doesn't synthesize disparate elements as much as he sets them up against each other and highlights the struggle. For a long time I believed that the authentic religious life was one of struggle, but I had never heard it so perfectly reproduced as music. And not only was it music, it was Jewish music to be sure.

There is a deep regard for tradition in this music as much as there is a responsibility to keep it new, to keep it modern. When Krakauer plays a standard klezmer *Nign*, a brooding song without words, and beneath it Ted Reichman's accordion pumps out atonal noise, you'd think the whole thing would buckle, then shatter, under the weight of the contradiction. But what holds it together is a sense of something transcendent. There is a reaching and a longing toward God, toward making this seeming contradictory noise mean something. Whatever the musicians' intent, it's about as religious as anything you'll ever hear, making audible an ancient tension between encountering God in tradition and seeking God in the contemporary.

Klezmer is traditionally secular music, but it imitates Jewish liturgical forms and creates a sense of spiritual worldliness. While it is music that can uplift and draw deep from emotional wells, it is not by default religious music. If anything, klezmer is earthly, fleshy. It's the music of daily encounters, and while formally played at weddings and other celebrations, it also contains the stories of these events—the emotions and the spirit. But klezmer is also a vessel for the ways in which the religious life interacts with the secular. Even more important, klezmer is a form of music that insists there is really no division. To be religious is to be in service of creation. This is what makes klezmer decidedly Jewish.

To encounter Judaism in culture, as opposed to the ritual, is an important part of what it means to be Jewish. Religion is often defined by theology and liturgy: the way people worship, what they believe, how they pray. But religious practice also happens outside the synagogue and the church. Religion binds people together by offering them a way to speak about their lives; it lives through the stories that they tell. In this sense, religion is more like a language than a set of beliefs. Religious life has a grammar, colloquialisms, and even slang. And where better to hear the actual sound that religion makes outside the temple than in the music on the street? It is in our daily lives that identity is more firmly constructed. It gets built out of the mortar and brick of family and, in my experience, stands up on a foundation of food, stories, jokes, and superstition.

There were some things we did that I knew were Jewish and that separated me from the other kids: the little bits of Yiddish spoken in our home, the brisket and kasha varnishkas on Rosh Hashanah, taking matzo to school during the Passover week. My mother lit the Sabbath candles with her hand pressed up above her eyes and she whispered something, the content itself her own secret, but still I was meant to hear her utter it. And we rarely spoke about being Jewish. This was something inherent to our state of being. But it wasn't synagogue that defined it for us. I grew up decidedly secular. Our Jewishness was in the stories we told about ourselves.

Klezmer also acts like a story, conjuring up images of Eastern Europe, of shuffling from country to country, gathering up culture and languages like a peasant picking vegetables at the market. And like any good story, it begins to take on the historical realities of where and when it is told. This is what religion does as it changes and adapts through time. My encounter with klezmer happened when musicians could understand it in a context that by then could draw upon a huge musical canvas. Punk rock, glam, surf and rockabilly, modern classical, and most important jazz—because of its already pliable and mercurial attributes—were folded into the fabric of a simple kind of folk music. Contemporary klezmer musicians don't have to abandon the new to get access to the old. In fact, the old is no longer a mere ghost haunting the edges of musical tradition when it becomes infused with modern musical language. The new sound is like a golem, in some ways an artificial construct but imbued with actual spirit. The clothing is a mishmash of clay and stone, sticks and mud. But the power that animates it is godly.

Can my faith be like this? Can I build something out of pieces of the old and the new? Or do I harm the foundation, making what rises eventually unstable, rickety? How much do I have to be beholden to tradition to call myself religious, to call myself a Jew? How much can the faith of forefathers sound a little like rock 'n' roll before it is no longer anything like what they believed? And yet, no matter what I have tried to clothe my faith in—from drug-addled mysticism to lighting Friday-night candles with my wife and son—God keeps playing the same song over and over again. It is the song I believe in. It is a song that is as old, probably older, than the psalm that tries to capture it:

> *The Lord is my shepherd, I shall not want.*
> *He makes me lie down in green pastures; He leads me beside*
> *   still waters;*
> *He restores my soul.*
> *He leads me in right paths for His name's sake.*

A clarinet is a scary-looking instrument, especially if you've never played any instrument before. It's a veritable puzzle to put together, and then, once whole, the number of keys and their odd placement looks almost otherworldly. After a while, though, when I held the clarinet, something about it began to make sense: the way it fit in my hand, my right thumb on the little metal rest, my other fingers hovering above the keys.

My teacher insisted that I not only learn how to read music but also practice rhythmic development without the instrument. This meant that every day I had to count out time along with a metronome by patting my knees with my palms. This was not what I had signed up for. This was turning into work. But despite myself, I practiced every day. I learned the notes and learned the keys and learned the rhythm charts. And like I often do, I became obsessed with the paraphernalia. I started spending time in music stores, buying sheet music, different brands of reeds, and electronic metronomes. But no matter how I tried, walking down the street with my little square clarinet case always made me feel self-conscious. And yet the idea that someone else who played the clarinet would see me was exciting. I wanted membership in this secret club.

Once, many years ago, I was on the bus reading the twelfth-century book of Jewish philosophy, Moses Maimonides' *Guide for the Perplexed*, a beautiful red hardcover edition, and who gets on the bus but a lumbering giant of an orthodox Jew, his wide-brimmed hat barely able to make it through the pneumatic door. He sat a few seats away from me and I could practically feel the book begin to vibrate. I half expected that he would somehow feel it also, this kind of Jewish energy suddenly a thread connecting us, me the teachable student, open and eager to learn from a master, from a *tzaddik!* My religious mind was still immature enough to think coincidence was the surest proof of the existence of God, so I was certain something was going to happen. Somehow he would just know that I was reading this classic of Jewish literature. But nothing did happen. Finding his seat, the Hasidic fellow didn't even turn to look at me, didn't even *notice* me.

I moved to the seat next to him and held out the book like a talisman, like a beacon. I may as well have thrown it at him for all my heart-pounding casualness. And then blubbering, I somehow got out a disjointed, but to my ears precious and earnest, explanation of how I had not grown up with very much religion and I was coming back to Judaism and look, see here, I really mean it, I am even reading Maimonides and would you be so kind as to pull God out from under your hat?

He limply shook my hand and, taking the book from me, turned it back and forth like it was a Christian tract he had found on the floor and wasn't sure how best to discard. Then with another wave of his hand he dismissed my searching, my yearning, and in so many words, scolded me for bothering with such a book, saying, "There is nothing for you to read but Torah."

For some reason I was not surprised by his reaction, but I was still disappointed. I wanted my own early religious fumblings to be taken seriously. I wanted permission to seek God in my own way but still be regarded as a Jew. I wanted my faith to make me like a Mason, where you know that there are others everywhere who are just like you, and if you flash the right hand gesture or carry the right book, you can wink knowingly and be on your way, secure in the knowledge that you are not alone.

Believing the clarinet made me part of a secret organization didn't get me any closer to learning how to play—just as wanting to appear faithful, wanting to display religiosity, however covertly to a chosen few, didn't make me any more religious. Simply wearing the costume doesn't make the actor the character. And yet the dressing is often the way in which faith is apprehended. A pure encounter with the holy, with the divine, is beyond language. Religion is the phenomenon of putting the encounter into identifiable terms through myth, symbol, ritual. In the book of Genesis, the patriarch Jacob has a dream in which angels are going up and down a ladder. After he wakes, he immediately sanctifies the moment by naming and ritualizing it: "He took the stone . . . and set it up for a pillar and poured oil on the top of it. He called the place Bethel [house of God]." While almost primitive, Jacob's response is authentic. In order not to forget, Jacob has to record it. He designates the place as holy and gives it a name.

The danger, I learned, is that someone seeing the stone will mistake it as being more valuable than the vision, or encounter, itself. I became too focused on what my faith looked like, rather than really building a temple to God in my heart, which I have found takes work.

A few months into clarinet lessons, my mother, Ruth, became ill with cancer. Within weeks, the change in my mother was so dramatic that my father thought she might be having an allergic reaction to the morphine. She was hallucinating and could barely stand on her own. She was folding into herself like a piece of cellophane being slowly heated. Everything happened so fast that it seemed as if we were all trying to hurry up and get the dying over with already because we couldn't take it anymore, couldn't stand to see her slowly wasting away. On the weekend before she died, I was sitting with her alone on the small couch across the room from her hospital bed. She was in a strange state, as if talking in her sleep, but was still able to see and hear everything that was going on. She recognized me, was happy to see me. Suddenly she pointed at the chrome bars of the bed and said, "Those are clarinet keys. Your clarinet keys."

These were among the last words she would ever say to me.

A few weeks before the news of her cancer, I had brought my clarinet over to my parents' house for the first time and played it for them. They were pleasantly supportive, as they had been my whole life regarding all of my many "hobbies," but I figured they didn't take it too seriously.

But she did. It was the lingering sound of my new clarinet that would be between us on her last days. Not God. We never talked about that. Not some religious wisdom from the depths of her unconscious, struggling to rise above a surface of hallucinations and dementia. But her words to me did come from somewhere deep. And not surprisingly, it was a place we shared most of all. My mother grew up in Brockton, a poor working-class town, south of Boston. But when she was old enough to have the means, whenever she was able she fled to Boston for one thing and one thing only: jazz.

Even as a teenager, when my musical tastes were becoming eclectic, I avoided jazz. It was my parents' music, music for adults. There were no guitars as far as I could tell. It was music to sip cocktails and dance slowly to. Nevertheless, I couldn't help but stumble upon jazz references and influences in my journeys around rock 'n' roll history. Jazz did not exist in the musical vacuum I had thought. Friends started lending me albums, Davis's *Kind of Blue*, Coltrane's *A Love Supreme*. Was this what my mother had been talking about all these years that I had so quickly dismissed?

Once in, I wanted to hear more. Soon, to my mother's delight, I discovered not only icons like Miles and Coltrane but also the guilty pleasures of the West Coast sound, performers like Stan Getz and Gerry Mulligan. These guys were not cool the way Coltrane and Miles were cool, but they were my mother's favorites. Their music was less introspective, more romantic. It was music for chasing girls and reading poetry and smoking cigarettes while you played chess.

In the few years before she got sick, my mother and I started talking about things in a way we never had. Through music. We would sit in her living room and sing standards together. She told me stories of the jazz clubs, of one night when, at closing time, she and some friends and the musicians all ordered Chinese food. After they ate, the band started up again and played until dawn. We had never connected like this before, and in fact many years between us had been strained when I was too stoned to care.

Beneath all the reminiscing I could glean what music really meant to my mother. For her, it was also a place to encounter the divine. Music—something so utterly human, made by human beings with human things—is a central means we use to "speak" about God. It is, like a psalm or Jacob's rock covered in oil, a way to communicate the incommunicable, the ineffable. For my mother, jazz was a path that led directly to her soul's longing for connection, to the meeting place between the holy and the mundane. It is no wonder the Jewish liturgy is sung, or that music has always played such a central role in religious worship. Music binds communities and the individuals in those communities, just as it bound me to my mother. Anne Lamott, in her spiritual memoir *Traveling Mercies* reflects on both the physical and religious connection that can happen between people with music: "Maybe it's because music is as physical as it gets: Your essential rhythm is your heartbeat, your essential sound, the breath. We're walking temples of noise, and when you add tender hearts to this mix, it somehow lets us meet in places we couldn't get to in any other way." Song expresses the most earthly thing, formed in our chests and in our throats. It then needs our tongues and our spit, our teeth and our lips. There is no way to make music, even the most religious music, without the body, the moist, fecund, fleshy body.

My mother embraced the things of the world. And even as she had a list of favorites—cigarettes, diamonds, romantic love, and old Hollywood movies—she loved jazz most of all because in its worldliness, it was the closest to God she could get.

At each lesson after my mother died—and really with all the music I listened to in my life—there was no song I played or listened to that didn't contain some element of spiritual ache. But I also heard in music the struggle against death, the struggle against certainty. Genuine faith means to live inside a place of extreme waiting, so extreme that it no longer even looks like waiting. It just looks like making music.

Over the next year I continued to practice and slowly grew more and more comfortable. But during one lesson my teacher pointed out that while I was becoming technically proficient, I was not putting any heart into my playing: I was not letting go. When she said this, I immediately realized there was a place in my playing I had not reached yet—that I was actually afraid. It felt again like that awful abyss into which, even today, my faith sometimes falls.

In what way was I unable to let go? Why in my life could I not fully believe? I could read the music. I knew where to place my fingers. And I earnestly wanted to play. But it seemed I had so long come to rely on doubt as an important function in my religious life that I had begun to doubt more than I believed. It was no longer a matter of discipline. I had overcome my fear of work and craft. I knew these things were not the stumbling block to freedom I once thought they were. I had long been afraid of discipline, of practice, of having to do something over and over again before I got it right. I had once thought that the only things that were meaningful were those that were discovered through inspiration, mystical awareness, and dramatic spiritual transformations. I hungered for these kinds of experiences, so much so that I became resistant to seeing that meaning was more often found in the mundane, in ritual and practice, in discipline and work.

At an earlier time in my life, the idea of learning how to play an instrument seemed pointless because I thought, unless I could immediately use the instrument as a tool for expression, for tuning into the music of the spheres, what, ultimately, was the point? An instrument took so much time to master. I would likely be dead before I could really play it. Yet as I continued to practice the clarinet, I was better able to understand that real freedom, real inspiration, was to be found in all the things that I thought would choke the life out of me: sobriety, monogamy, craft, and practice.

But still I knew my doubt more intimately. In doubt there is an odd kind of certainty. It's like riding a bike. You *could* fall at any moment, but it also feels impossible to fall. The thing that keeps you up is the same thing that can knock you down. But also in doubt there is no real risk. Risk involves letting go of doubt and moving fully into faith, where the greatest risk lies. What if I am wrong? What if I make a fool of myself? What if it sounds awful? What if God is not what I had hoped after all?

Ironically, letting go is its own kind of discipline. The discipline it takes to really play an instrument is similar to the discipline it takes to believe in God. I am not referring to observance—the practice of religion—necessarily, although it is one way in which discipline in matters of faith can and sometimes must manifest itself. The discipline of faith is one whereby I continue to take the risk and make a commitment to an ultimate reality. The anthropologist Mircea Eliade defines religion as the belief in an "absolute reality, the sacred, which transcends this world but manifests itself in this world, thereby sanctifying it and making it real." More than belief, religion, according to Eliade, is the "reactualizing" of myth, of the stories, in our lives. It is the encounter with religious language through prayer, contemplation, dialogue, meditation, ritual, and liturgy, which is the lived expression of this belief. And music, another expression of religious language, also involves risk. There is nothing more open-ended than learning how to play an instrument. There is no final goal, no perfect realization. This discipline is even more difficult in the actual dailiness of life, in relationships with other people, in ethical behavior, in simply doing what I believe God would want me to do.

Religious people often speak of "God's will" as if it is something that God does to us. My encounters with God involve not my having to respond to some chess move on God's part, but on a demand that I believe God makes of me to live and act in a particular way. To live in holiness is not to be holy, but to struggle with the demand of what God would have me be. And as with the clarinet, it takes practice. Practice and more practice. Learning how to do God's will requires the same perseverance as learning how to play an instrument. The technical aspects of the clarinet are only a part of what it takes. It also takes patience and focus—not allowing myself to get distracted by other things, or as the psalmist might say, other gods:

> *I waited patiently for the Lord;*
> *He inclined to me and heard my cry.*
> *He drew me up from the desolate pit,*
> *out of the miry bog, and set my feet upon a rock,*
> *making my steps secure.*

He put a new song in my mouth,
a song of praise to our God . . .
Happy are those who make
the Lord their trust,
Who do not turn to the proud,
to those who go astray after false gods. (Psalm 40)

This psalm warns against immediate spiritual understanding, instead entreating that we wait "patiently for the Lord." It also means I'm not going to be able to play like Krakauer after a few lessons, if ever.

In both Christianity and Judaism there exists the desire for an ultimate conclusion to faith, for an end to all the stumbling. The Christian version has infused itself much more deeply in the popular imagination, and there is an entire market driven by eschatological belief, with books, both fiction and nonfiction, and film and even popular music. The return of the messiah is understood by many as an actual future occurrence that will end the world as we know it, separate true believers from nonbelievers, and herald in a new age with Jesus as the reigning king.

Jewish messianism takes many different forms, including secular and liberal approaches that are concerned with radical social and political change to ensure the survival of Judaism and the universalizing of its ethics and religious values. Nevertheless, in orthodox terms, the desire for an ultimate transformative event resulting in the crowing of a king still plays an important role in the theological underpinnings, particularly within the Hasidic movement. What is dangerous about these ideas is that in the rush toward the end-time—in our impatience—what needs attending to now can be lost. It is also dangerous because it means that each historical moment is read as a signpost on the road toward this final destination. It makes it harder to have compassion for earthquake victims when you believe the earthquake was preordained and is heralding something you are actually looking forward to, the Big Earthquake that you pray for, that you ache for, because it means God will be standing upon the rubble, flaming sword in hand. It also means that faith is an equation that will one day be solved, rather than a series of encounters with the holy.

Faith is not like a song with a beginning, middle, and end. Faith is the whole musical scale, an endless and infinite series of permutations of notes. When faith is about practicing our moral obligations, then the community of human beings becomes much more precious. If anything, I want to stave off the end of the world as long as possible, because when we get there, it will be more likely that we've done it to ourselves. To sacrifice the belief in some final answer is scary and allows doubt to creep in.

Letting go means trusting that God will pull me up from the pit of doubt. But it also means I must believe even in the midst of doubt, must pray even when it feels as though I am praying to the void, to what Hemingway's waiter in "A Clean, Well-Lighted Place" calls *"Nada y pues nada y pues nada."* It means practicing the clarinet even when it sounds like crap.

At the next lesson, I tried to forget about "playing" the clarinet and trusted that I had learned enough for some of it to become second nature. Now I could try to just make some music. It was like the first lesson all over again. I was sweating and nervous. I was embarrassed for both not being able to do it and for even try-ing. But I could feel the longing inside me. It was that old ache again, the yearning for something beyond myself to apprehend me, the yearning to experience transcendence. I had become so fixed on the discipline, so afraid of that part of me that wanted something mystical because that had always been the part that had gotten me into trouble. Here I was again, not satisfied. But something was different. My desire had a foundation of practice and patience. I had waited this time. I had not looked for the quick fix in a hit of acid or a fleeting romance. So I put the clarinet to my lips, let my doubt and my faith stare each other down, and I made some music. I stomped my feet and swayed my head. I blew into that horn and heard something I had never really heard before. I think they call it religion.

Before I had even heard Krakauer, my whole life had been preparing me for the moment when I would let go enough to take the risk to learn how to play the clarinet. Looking back, I saw that the risk had always been there in the music I'd listened to before—and in the way I lived, the things I had done, the people I had known. I came to the clarinet by way of punk rock, drugs, mysticism, sobriety, prayer, and marriage, each forming a part of the clarinet: mouthpiece, ligature, barrel, upper joint, lower joint, and bell. I came to the clarinet much in the same way I came to understand God. I stumbled—oh, how I stumbled. But I kept getting up.

I continued to practice until the arrival of my son made it much more difficult. That extra half hour once devoted to the clarinet was now used for playing with Samuel, quick naps, cleaning the house, doing laundry. But I'm not sure I would have known how to do these things if not for the clarinet. I am not sure I would have had the patience and the focus it takes to really be a new parent.

The clarinet is now under my bed in its hard case. The last time I took it out was to show my son, and while I could get a few notes out of it, the sound was a little shrill and whiny. After I let him fiddle with it for a few minutes, I took it apart, laid each piece in its little felt bed, and closed it up like a coffin. I put it back under my bed. I know it's there. I sense it every day. I hear it. It plays the same song over and over again. It's a song that lifts and swells. It's a song that scares me and gives me hope. It is the song of angels ascending and descending, a song of heaven and earth. The clarinet plays the song of my faith.

EPILOGUE
— SK —

Though I once noticed the case under Peter's bed while playing hide-and-seek with his son, Sam, I've never actually seen the clarinet. He's never assembled it for me in a nostalgic moment remembering his mom. I've never heard him practice from the other room. He rarely ever mentions it or his awkward and sweaty moments learning to play.

During my visits to Cambridge, though, just as soon as he and Amy have put Sam to bed, Peter sits me down on the couch for a different kind of music lesson. One he's much more comfortable with. It's the one thing we're sure to do every time we see each other. He plays me something I've never heard before. Once it was King Crimson's 1970 *In the Wake of Poseidon*, and later the Kinks' *Village Green Preservation Society*, recorded two years earlier, he tells me. We've listened to both the Beta Band and the Incredible String Band. And there's always been another brand-new album to get through, some contemporary psychedelic folk music that recalls those early days with the late Beatles and Donovan. Usually there is one song in particular that he's been playing over and over all week. That's the one we focus on.

Peter insists that when we listen to music together, we really listen. "Put your feet up," he says. "Close your eyes."

He puts the CD on and turns the volume up as loud as he can, which is always louder than I expect with his son sleeping in the other room, and the first time through any song we don't say a word. I know he'll play it again and really walk me through it.

He's like a wiser older brother in this respect, more patient than me, a quality that probably comes with age and difficult experiences with good music. When I play music for him, I'm liable to skip ahead to the middle of a song, rewind over and over again to hear just a favorite few seconds, or switch albums after the first couple tracks. When I grew antsy like this as a kid, my stepfather, who was reliably slow in everything but leaving the house Sunday mornings for church, had a favorite saying: "Patience is a blessed virtue." And in that first listen through any song, Peter proves him right, and the music blesses us.

Now, I'm no slouch when it comes to music. Our first shared love—before Flannery O'Connor and way before God—was the droning and hypnotic 1998 album *In the Aeroplane Over the Sea* by psych-folk band Neutral Milk Hotel. I may have come late to artists like Dylan, Tyrannosaurus Rex, and the Troggs, but—with help from my friends—I feel like I've arrived all the same. Just like a kid brother. Still, Peter's experience seems far deeper than mine, somehow worthier now for the spiritual battles that accompanied his first experiences with the Who and Pink Floyd and the inscrutable sexuality of Bowie, Iggy Pop, and Queen. He's a more avid and curious fan, just as he's always been a more avid and curious believer. His practiced appreciation of music is what remains of the very serious troubles Peter faced growing up, troubles that I studiously and piously avoided.

Unlike my actual older brother—whom I love, don't get me

wrong, but whose taste in music has gone from bad to worse in the last twenty years, and never really included even the Beatles—Peter has something to teach me about music. And as often as he tells me about bands I've never heard of, we experience together the lesson he learned from his mother: Music is the divine place where we meet.

When I open my eyes, he starts the song over. The second time through he tells me what to listen for. *This part really swells. Listen.*

And after the song swells, he closes his eyes, and for the last few years I've always imagined him at twelve again, when he first played Eric's records. At home here, I think about Sam—like the younger brother I never had, like a nephew—fast asleep in the other room after our day of hide-and-seek. Sitting next to me, Peter seems just as peaceful. But as the song swells again, he flinches, and I'm sure he's not.

Peter calls me almost every day, although never before eight in the morning. On Tuesday, July 13, 2004, I'd gotten up early and by seven had made it to a local café, where I was then in the habit of doing the *New York Times* crossword before eight o'clock Mass at the church across the street. Tuesday crosswords are easy, and I'd filled it in by the time Peter called around seven thirty.

His older brother Eric, Sam's uncle, suffering a debilitating depression, had killed himself the night before. It was the first I'd ever heard of Eric's sickness. Peter didn't offer many details, just that he learned around one in the morning, and Amy had kept him from calling then. The news would be no different when they woke up.

He wanted to talk while Sam was still asleep. Often distracted and rushed during our conversations, with his son begging for his attention, this morning Peter hoped to be able to take his time. He wanted to connect—with me, with God, and with Eric. We muddled through. And this conversation, a mix of sorrow and comfort, regret and hope, silence and a burst of tears, felt just like prayer and was a perfect expression of our faiths.

I never met Eric. And apart from Peter's stories about music, I still know very little about him. Peter promises to tell me everything someday, although part of his silence—part of his regret, I think—has to do with the fact that he barely knew Eric either.

So there may never be much more than the music.

There are two things, though, that Peter found worth mentioning, but couldn't for a full year after the fact. In an e-mail dated July 12, 2005, Peter wrote that he and Eric had become very close in the weeks surrounding the death of their mother, Ruth, mostly, it seems, because Eric became an older brother again, although Peter's been vague: "Eric was a rock, a real support for all of us, and went above and beyond in taking care of so many details and day-to-day things that needed attending." More memorable than anything else, though, was Eric's relationship with Sam. Apparently he was a good uncle, and so a good brother:

> The time when I saw Eric shine the most, when I saw him
> the happiest and the most relaxed, the most truly himself,
> was with Sam . . . He was just this great fun funny man
> and Sam really loved him. There was a day that Eric and
> [his wife] Cheryl were coming over, and when they rang the
> bell, Sam literally jumped up and down. Sam still asks
> about him, and he poses some hard questions about death.
> (He recently asked if there were toilets in heaven.) I don't
> think I ever felt closer to my brother than around Sam.

Early in her autobiography, *The Long Loneliness*, Catholic writer Dorothy Day admits, "going to confession is hard." Comparing confession with writing, Day blames the difficulty on how each practice involves "giving yourself away." "But," she concludes, "if you love, you want to give yourself." After Eric died, Peter experienced the sort of loneliness that makes Catholic confession hard, the long loneliness that descends when we realize we are "separated from [our] fellows." Sin, often described as the separation from God, is not so different. In fact, if God may be found in our love for others, loneliness and sin could be considered the very same thing. And sin, like loneliness, would always be better handled through love and sympathy than punishment.

This is the hope for confession and prayer, to sympathize with the sinner.

Likewise, music can bring us closer; it, too, keeps us from loneliness. So we overcome our loneliness together. And it is hard.

For most of my life, though, where God was concerned I delighted in being alone, which meant I was special and chosen. Perhaps I'd always found confession simply too hard. Giving myself away to anyone else when God would willingly have me— for years he seemed to be calling me by name—seemed like a poor alternative.

Only now, years later, it strikes me: How sad to think that a long loneliness once felt to me like a religious calling. In the conversation with Peter after his brother died was the sad reminder that at one point in my life—the very moment I believed myself ready to give my life to God, answering his call to be a priest—I actually had no idea about love.

"Scott," he said. "Even though he was surrounded by people, Eric was just so alone."

And Peter knew that this would resonate with me. Descending into loneliness had always been my greatest sin.

Solitude is no place to find God. That's why we listen to music together. That's why Peter calls.

THE PRIEST

— SK —

AFTER YEARS OF PRAYING for it, the call finally came in late February 1994, when I was seventeen. This seemed like perfect timing. And after mulling it over for a few days, I decided a fire in the fireplace would help set a warm enough mood to tell my parents what God had decided would become of me. Ever since my days lighting candles and burning incense as an altar boy, fires had seemed holy and reassuring.

This would be the holiest day of my life.

If only I could have assured them I'd be a doctor someday, there'd have been no risk of anyone getting hurt. Weeks earlier, my mother had taken a look at my nimble fingers and perfect grade-point average and suggested I consider pediatric heart surgery. But I was too good for that. I was too good for a normal life. Too good to have a family or a job to support one. Too good to have my own house, my own yard, my own life. And, undoubtedly, too scared for all that as well. Because the odds were never good when you thought about it. I wanted to be a wild success. And just how many wild successes could this little town produce?

I always assumed there would be no professional athletes to emerge from the ball fields or playgrounds of Waterford's local schools and parks. Not only was the talent pool limited by a tiny population, preventing the kinds of intersquad challenges and one-upmanship that make good players great, but in my corner of rural Wisconsin, where the winters are very cold and the families solidly middle-class, year-round play and coaching are impossible. In our schools, no one struck me as inventive enough to make good on his scientific imagination or skills at math. The closest to genius I'd encountered was the PhD engineer from down the block who'd gone on to produce tastier jams and jellies for a food and chemical company in Minnesota. She'd not only gotten out of town but had actually fled the state. But since she caused her parents grief by waiting so long to get married, and her brother had recently been arrested on drug charges, that family seemed less than blessed.

Growing up, no one seemed beautiful enough for Hollywood or smart enough for Harvard. No one was ambitious enough for Washington or savvy enough for Wall Street.

For my part, I was thinking Nazareth and Rome, if only to be sure I was good and scared enough for heaven. As a priest, I could be assured the greatest success imaginable.

Boy, was I ever good and scared. And my parents, better than anyone else, knew just how good and just how scared I was—and just how I'd gotten that way. I was counting on them to understand when I broke the news that they'd have to rely on Frank and Sara for their grandchildren. This detail hardly mattered to me. I was too good and too scared for sex. I'd give up chasing girls and welcome the vow of celibacy. On that count, so far I was doing just fine; chasing girls had never come to more than a hand down the pants. It would be a small sacrifice to abandon that forever. And with no more fear of rejection, no more jealousies and no more risk of sin, celibacy would, in fact, be a great relief. After tonight, there would be no more deliberations. I would never be a doctor. I would be, as we knew from church, *forever virgin*. Like Mary. And better, like Christ.

My mind was made up—or rather, God's was. My parents had a young priest on their hands. And as Catholics, we believed that every priest had been called by name—I'd heard a version of *"Scott, Scott!"*—to serve God as a leader in his church. To work in a church and be supported by it. To live in a house next to that church where the yard was everyone's. To be without a wife or children, and, it seemed to me, without friends. After all, who could be friends with a priest? And whom could a priest be friends with? Who was good enough? Our priest greeted us when we left the church, then ducked away into the vestry. In town he was always alone in his collar, buying groceries for one. The man was always a priest.

Certain Catholics, like me, have tended to see their priests as aloof, mad scientists. Although to a certain extent one can hardly blame them: It's difficult to expect anyone to see priests as anything else, what with the model of priestliness being the maddest and aloofest miracle worker ever.

St. Thomas Aquinas was the namesake of my childhood church. Together with Saints Paul and Augustine, Aquinas has all but defined what it is to be Catholic, and is perhaps the most clear about the way Catholics ought to view the relationship between Christ and his priests: "Christ is the source of all priesthood: The priest of the old law was a figure of Christ, and the priest of the new law acts in the person of Christ." And in the way it presents Jesus, the Gospel of John basically shapes the way that I imagined the priestly life should be lived. John's Gospel is at once the most beautiful and the most peculiar, different than Matthew, Mark, and

Luke, known as the synoptic Gospels, which cover mainly the same ground. John comes from a different planet.

The book of Mark, written in the sixties A.D., is the shortest and crudest of the Gospels, and was a source for the writers of Matthew and Luke, both written near the end of the first century, each of which added birth narratives, included collections of sayings not found in Mark, and developed a fuller Resurrection myth. In Matthew and Luke, Jesus is born in a barn. He delivers long and famous sermons on a Mount and on a Plain that become the core of his ministry. Mark's Jesus performs miracles and then insists that no one say a word. In the synoptics, Jesus is noted for teaching through earthy parables and often seems unknowing or reticent about his relationship to God the Father.

Jesus of John's Gospel, however, very often plays what might be called the spiritual monologist, claiming his role in the whole cosmic story of creation, insisting over and over on his oneness with God. Only once does Jesus even get his hands dirty, spitting in the dust and spreading mud on the eyes of a blind man to restore his sight. Even when Jesus gets up to wash the feet of the apostles at supper the evening before Passover, John reminds us that Jesus "had come from God and was going to God." Jesus turns the whole washing into a spiritual exercise, a sort of baptism: "Unless I wash you," he says to Peter, "you have no share with me." And Judas, the lone unclean apostle, isn't guilty of tracking in mud, but is pegged by John as the one who will betray his teacher and Lord by turning him over to the soldiers and police sent by the chief priests and Pharisees. In the synoptics, Jesus is betrayed with a kiss from Judas. In John, Judas, standing with a group of soldiers, doesn't even get close. Jesus gives himself up by echoing God from the Old Testament and claiming his divinity: "*I am He.*" And when the apostle Simon Peter tries to defend Jesus by cutting off the right ear of the high priest's slave, in the Gospels of Luke and Matthew, Jesus heals the slave by touching him; in John, Jesus ignores the bleeding slave and scolds Peter for trying to stand in the way of his otherworldly destiny—"Put your sword back into its sheath. Am I not to drink the cup that the Father has given me?" We're led to expect this in John, where Jesus' soul is too good to be true.

This was my model of the priestly life; these perfect yearnings of John's otherworldly Jesus shaped my calling. He possesses—I know now—what the German Romantics called the "beautiful soul," the impossible ideal of consistency and constancy among mind, body, and spirit. He never falters, never gives in to temptation. He is not ambitious. He is never sullied by the world. His commitments are never exclusive. His soul is just too beautiful.

And this was the model of Jesus that tempted me to develop a character—a soul—that could, as the Romantic Friedrich von Schiller put it, "allow the passions to guide its will without worry, because there is never a danger that there will be a contradiction with its decisions." If Jesus, who for Christians is known as the Word, and God are one, as John's Gospel claims in its opening lines—*In the beginning was the Word, and the Word was with God, and the Word was God*—then Jesus' passions and God's will must also be one, and contradiction between them impossible. This was the ideal of a priestly life: a man who is one with God and unsullied by the world.

I would give up a life of choices and contradictions, of friends and family, for the life God had chosen for me. I'd always wear black. I might never get my hands dirty. I'd had nothing to do with it, already had no choice in the matter. Like Jesus, who at thirteen was already teaching among the rabbis in the temple, which he knew instinctually to be his Father's house, I'd been born this way. Who was I to say no?

Almost immediately, Mary and Joseph had conceded that God's

work would be done through their son. They knew even before he was born that they had a special boy. And according to the church, priests were like Jesus' brothers, acting in the person of Christ. As I saw it, all Christians may have been chosen, but priests were chosen for more special work. All Christians may have been good, but priests, they were simply better. All Christians may have lived with the fear of God, but priests were just more scared. All Christians would face God someday alone, but priests would always be lonelier. In me, I thought God had chosen particularly well: a special, better, scared, and lonely young man.

I didn't suppose I would be asking my parents for their blessings that night so much as telling them what God had quietly been telling me. Had I been asking for permission, my parents might have said no. They had often said no to me. But no way could they say no to God.

Yet leading up to this night, I must have figured they'd try to disagree. They would not trust me. They would not understand. I should have been more confident. I should have had more faith. Because, on what was supposed to be an occasion even more momentous than announcing your plans to be married, or telling your parents that they would soon be grandparents, I was expecting an argument. As if they knew I'd chosen the wrong woman or just knocked up some girl from school. As if somehow they knew this wife would soon leave me.

But at the time I was good and scared and seventeen. Announcing anything at all made me nervous.

"I'm going out for some wood," I said. And I went out into the dark of my backyard.

My parents would have to admit this was largely their doing. Any misunderstandings, disappointments, and hurt feelings that would come of this night in February would be largely their fault. They might have expected it—perhaps they did—because together they raised me a faithful Catholic.

Admittedly, lots of children are brought up religious. My church was full of them, squawking and carrying on. Babies crying and rocked to sleep by their fathers in the vestibule. Altar boys and girls lighting incense and candles, looking pious in their white robes tied with white cords. A few others in the pews leaning against their mothers and nodding off. Some of the smallest ones eating tiny handfuls of Cheerios.

Yet of my parents' three kids, those of every other family in the parish, and even among the other acolytes, as a young boy only I'd ever demonstrated having memorized the whole Mass. By seven or eight, I would mutter along with the priest under my breath from Luke's Gospel—*This is my body which is given for you; do this in remembrance of me*—while the rest of the congregation bowed their heads in appropriate silence. Even most of the children followed suit, bowing. The priest held high the bread. Tiny bells were rung. And I became a special part of the mystery as bread became the body of Christ. Still, whenever I helped the priest like this, with the miracle of transubstantiation, by praying his prayer out loud with him, my mother would turn, look low, and shush me for speaking out of turn. In time I had to learn to keep my voice down because there was never any stopping those words from running through my head. There still isn't.

Together, week after week, we kneeled and sat and stood as Catholics do, developing muscle memory to accompany the prayers through a kind of holy calisthenics, repeating every week from the pews, *Lord, I am not worthy that you should enter under my roof, but only say the word and I shall be healed.*

Healed? Were we sick? Broken? Did we *need* to be healed?

Of course we did. At the very least, each of us was born with original sin; when Adam and Eve had disobeyed God in the Garden of Eden, they'd fallen, and somehow we'd all fallen with them. Not only that, but we fell again every day, somehow, all on our own. There was no use denying it. Even the priest, God's spokesman and Jesus' brother, admitted, *Lord, we have sinned against you. Lord, have mercy.* "We," he'd say every week, meaning him, too. I mumbled along with those lines, *his* lines, and then kept right on talking, joining the congregation in their response: *Lord, have mercy.* A few times a year we went to confession, sat alone in a box with a priest on the other side of a screen, and really laid it on the line: I swore at my brother. I cheated on a test. I thought about a girl and played with myself. And I was forgiven. As a family, every Sunday we received the Eucharist, that body given for us and transformed in front of us with my help—what Saint Ignatius called the *medicine of immortality.*

So as sinners we exercised. We asked for mercy. We took our medicine. Not only would our lives be long, but if we kept this up, they could last forever. We were all betting on it.

Mine was always a fairly healthy religious family. I kept from sinning too much by doing my chores with hardly a complaint; I believed in God. I behaved and knew the commandments. I did not steal. I did not kill. I honored my father and mother. I didn't commit adultery. Neither did I covet any goats. And above all I loved God with all my heart, with all my mind, and with all my soul.

I studied very hard in school and prayed even harder in church. For years. And so not only was I good but, by Ignatius's account, I might also be well. The difference between the two—*good* and *well*—I had learned in school as a matter of grammar, and as a Catholic I needed to be both. Goodness itself was no mystery; Catholics believed in charity, in freely performing works that were good. I did my best around the house, say. Goodness, then, put us in the right state to be made well. We were ultimately healed—what Christians call *justified*—through the mystery of God's grace. And some day we would all go to heaven. Forever.

Of course, my parents were very good themselves—good, good models. My stepfather, Paul, a Catholic who'd married my mother a few years after a car accident killed my father, had met her through church connections—my father's sister had introduced them, in fact. A manager of a series of family-owned retail stores and, now, when I was seventeen, employed by Sears, in his free time Paul had always managed a diocese of thrift stores for a Catholic charity, the Society of Saint Vincent de Paul.

As usual, after we ate that night—reclining, digesting, performing charity in front of the TV—he flipped through his Society folders, taking notes. My first paid job as a writer was to compose their monthly newsletters; he'd just paid me out-of-pocket again for February. I felt rich.

My mother, Virginia, known as Ginger, who'd raised three children on her own in the years between the accident and her marriage to Paul, was a teacher who fed her children and protected them. Not usually charitable in the ways my stepdad was—in fact, my mother would often complain when he'd rush off to a church meeting in the evening—she never missed a school play or concert, a tennis match or an awards banquet, and was on call every evening to teach a lesson in history or explain how x could possibly ever equal y. In other words, the cliché had its proof in my mother: Charity began at home. It's no wonder building a fire to warm the house could make me feel a little holy.

She had just come downstairs in her nightgown and curled up on the couch.

They'd heard the back door slam. We kept the wood, piled up alongside the house every year around my birthday in early September, under a tarp to keep the snow off. My family lived at the middle of a winding subdivision of cul-de-sacs where most everyone had put up a fence to keep kids from drowning in the neighborhood pools, and along those fences were countless cords of wood. Our chimneys smoked all winter.

I took my time making the perfect stack in the fireplace. It was my nature to take my time and make things perfect—in this case, the perfect fire. It was my job, household work. I had to do it right. I had to do everything right. It kept me from sinning. It became meditative like prayer, just what I needed. I had a lot on my mind.

The underlying question facing everyone I knew at that age, the implication of college-recruitment mailings piling up on the desk in the dining room and the persistent, nagging whisper that kept my friends awake at night, was: *What will you make of yourself?*

And where parents were concerned, most everyone I knew was in the business of either pleasing or rebelling. On the face of it, I knew my business—the news I was preparing to deliver as I built this fire—might seem like rebellion to them.

But God had looked at my beautiful soul and not my skinny fingers. He'd listened, but never scolded, as I demonstrated for him each week in church just how prepared I already was—that I'd known all my lines, that I'd need no prompting as a priest.

What would I make of myself? I thought. Not a thing. I'd never have to. I'd vow to be poor and celibate like Jesus, because God himself had made me that way.

The flame took, and I finally told my mom I didn't think I'd make a very good doctor.

Smoke began to fill the family room. I had forgotten to open the flue.

The family room, with the floating ottoman and my stepdad's abused recliner, had always been where these serious conversations started. Just after moving in, we'd taken down the dark wood paneling and torn out the maroon shag carpet to lighten up the place and exorcise the ghosts of the previous owners, whom we knew to be, at the very least, hot-tempered, if the haunting fist holes in my closet doors upstairs were any indication. My stepfather tended to a tropical fish tank and my sister had a parakeet, and the two kept each other company in an endless hum of gurgles and chirps. The room was alive.

The family room was where, one summer morning in 1986, sitting cross-legged inches from the television, I'd finally asked my parents about AIDS and was assured that, no, I was not possibly infected. For one thing, I was only nine, my mom said. And there would be no second thing. She trailed off, dropping the subject because the things that made high-risk groups "high-risk" were not appropriate to talk about in front of the children. So I leaned in and learned from the newsman what a condom was.

The family room, with its ceiling fan and the Dutch door leading to the backyard, was also where, in the seventh grade, I'd failed to convince my parents that quitting the basketball team did not make me a quitter. I'd made my case about not playing enough, about the way the other kids treated me, and was driven back to practice the next week, where I offered a public apology for storming out in the first place. For kicking the ball across the gym. For telling Mike Axelson to fuck off.

In a related discussion just a few weeks later: Quitting public school was also out of the question, and not just because private school was too expensive, which it was. My mother was a public school teacher, and my father had been too, she reminded me. And in her experience, your average Catholic school kid could certainly be as mean as any public school kid. It didn't matter where a middle-school athlete spent his days learning; he would still let me know I was neither tall nor a particularly good shot, hardly a natural athlete. Regardless of the injustice of it, if some boy thought I'd cost us the game with an errant pass or a double dribble, no way Jesus was going to stop him from hurling the ball in the direction of my head just as Mike had.

And here we were again. I'd switched on the fan. I stood at the door waving my arms, apologizing to my parents for smoking them out. My mom sat there, coughing just as she had those years ago when she was still smoking, when she sat on that same couch denying me a Catholic education and advising me on how kids everywhere could be jerks.

Of course, back then she'd been right about Catholic kids. Over time, they had proved to be just as sinful as the people I went to school with across town. A neighbor had been the one encouraging me to join him at St. Thomas Aquinas school; yet we first talked about it one afternoon while hunting around the rafters of his parents' basement for stashes of his father's *Playboy*s. A few years later, a teenage cousin of mine, a Catholic schoolgirl, arrived at my grandmother's funeral Mass unmarried and pregnant; the buzz among the relatives was that my grandmother was already rolling over, even before the grave. And like my mom—a parochial schoolgirl herself—Catholic kids started smoking cigarettes at the same rate as anyone else I knew; and those burnouts gathered behind Dumpsters and off in the woods taking their first hits of pot that summer were not just the students whose education was covered by the taxpayers.

Until now it had been easy for my parents to point out the mistakes I'd made trying to plan a life for myself. In case after case—almost always in the family room—it had been easy for them to say no to a child. Even at seventeen, almost an adult, I never blamed them for disappointing me. They'd always been right to tell me no. But now, "No" would be impossible. And if they said it, I faced actually losing them. In the Gospels, Jesus says that we must hate our parents in order to follow him. But until that moment I had no idea what he meant. And I worried I wouldn't have it in me to hate them—nor to believe that God could be wrong in telling me that I needed to.

In the year before he died, my dad apparently noticed some potential in his second son. He sat me on his lap in a plush yellow chair in the living room and taught me to read through sheer repetition. He read and I memorized stories about Dick, Jane, and Spot word for word, and then finally looked at the page and realized that those arrangements of letters meant what I already knew to be true: I saw Dick go. I saw Jane go. *Go, go, go!* And for a short while at that age, reading alone was what set me apart. I impressed my teachers and made my parents proud. Everyone could run and nap and make noises on the Autoharp, and most could sing the ABCs along with the tune hammered out on the bells. But more impressive was being able to make something of the alphabet song, which meant being able to piece together the note pinned to your coat before mom even saw it.

It was through reading that I'd discovered my motto, some light verse—easily memorized—forged on a small iron wall hanging in the office of my grandparents' house. Removing it from the wall and feeling its weight at some point during each visit, I'd sit with it on my lap, read it over a few times, and replace it until it became as familiar as "See Dick go" and as meaningful as "Lord have mercy." And like the telephone numbers of grammar-school friends I could dial up today without a moment's pause, more than twenty years later, that motto still rattles off the tongue:

> *Good, better, best,*
> *Never let it rest,*
> *Until your good is your better,*
> *And your better is your best.*

I liked to be good. Or not just good, but always better, categorically better. Even way back then.

At school we played tag, and our giant first-grade teacher, at least six foot six and lean, was always the object of every pursuit. And those who were not as good at the game as I was, who didn't seem to understand the rules, hovered around him even when he was It, screaming as he got close, running in circles around his legs, leaping over each other just to be near him and the danger of becoming It. But the object of the game was to stay free. So in the warmer months, on days we'd play tag, I'd hide away in the bottom of the playground equipment—alone and nervous and quiet. In the winter I'd duck behind a snowbank piled up against the side of the building, watching the game from a safe distance, and hum to myself a TV-style theme song that celebrated my excellence at the game—another motto, another prayer:

> *This is the great escape,*
> *This is the great escape,*
> *This is the greatest escape in the world!*

I was never tagged. I was never It. Most days I was never seen. I had escaped.

It was then, as the best reader and the best game player, that I first felt chosen. And as my faith has evolved over the years, as doubt has crept in and I've responded as a Catholic to an entrenched and lately scandalous church, nothing—neither specific beliefs about the divinity of Jesus nor my practice of daily or weekly Mass—has had the religious impact that this sense of standing alone, uniquely and almost perfectly, before God has. I struggle with it to this day.

But as Christians, we were made to feel that way. We were good and better and best. The same precociousness that made my parents and teachers proud also had to endear me to God. Because I could read, I had learned to follow along in the missal before anyone else. I played the church game better. I ran my fingers along the readings selected from the Bible, recited the prayers, and sang at the top of my squeaky soprano's lungs, sure that I was delighting the adults around me, not to mention God, with piety.

In church, I both marked the passage of time and learned that time meant nothing compared with eternity. From line to line, reading to reading, hymn to hymn, Sunday to Sunday—Ordinary Time to Lent to Easter to Ordinary Time to Advent to Christmas—I moved through the year and became someone special, part of something larger than my country church in rural Wisconsin. One of the saved. The Bible told me as much. My parents told me as much. And the priest, the most special one in the church—the leader of all these chosen people—told me as much. And I could begin to help him because I knew all the words.

Someday I could be him.

The smoke had all cleared out and cold air from outside had rushed in. But the fire had warmed the room back to a comfortable temperature, and I sat cross-legged, like a child, on the ottoman.

"Mom and Dad," I said. "I have to tell you something." I had their attention. They waited.

At seventeen, I wanted to believe that I was called and chosen and special, and those things alone. The sense was actually not so different as when I was four, or six, or thirteen. Only now that I was old enough to ask what I might make of my life—and expected to have some idea—I could answer the call to the priesthood.

Scott, Scott! I'd heard.

Here I am, Lord. Sign me up, I was ready to say.

But what had always made this calling real was not just the piety I felt, or the feelings of superiority I had had since I first learned to read. No, I also had come to believe sadness was an essential part of a religious life. No one who had ever served God ever seemed particularly happy about it. All the best people—the saints, the prophets and martyrs, Jesus himself—suffered mightily. Happily, I thought all my loneliness had made me sufficiently sad. The appeal of the priesthood was a solitude I was already familiar with.

Priests were a category unto themselves. The Franciscan monastery on the edge of town was idyllic and mysterious, a community of priests living in the model of St. Francis, nature's patron saint. A Catholic version of Doctor Doolittle, a favorite character from my days reading my grandparents' Children's Classics collection, Francis of Assisi had miraculously talked with the animals. During the summers my family would drive out to the Franciscans' open-air chapel, where these good-natured monks in their brown hoods and sandals appeared to step out from a silent life spent among the pines to offer Mass for us, only to disappear again into the wilderness when it was ended. Those Sundays

I wanted to join them after the service, to wander off into the woods where God wanted me.

They must have had special prayers. I dreamed of wearing their hoods. St. Francis, or God himself, might have been out in those woods, teaching the monks the language of the animals.

But my flirtation with the Franciscans ended the afternoon I buried a small, bloodied blackbird in the backyard after shooting it out of a maple tree at twenty yards. I'd fired from the back door, safely out of the neighbors' sights, expecting the broad leaves to knock down my shot. When the bird fell, its wings and beak and legs getting momentarily hung up on the branches all the way down, I gasped—thrilled and sickened and guilty. I hid my BB gun and retrieved the shovel from the garage. I dug a shallow grave right where the bird had fallen, and covered its red guts, which bulged through the hole I'd made with my BB. In my panic—the bird had to be buried before my mother got home from work, and before my sister caught on from inside the house— I'd failed to make any ritual gesture over the bird, said no prayer, asked no forgiveness. My stepfather's St. Francis statue, however, its base damaged from scrapes with the lawn mower, made the perfect headstone. And although I'd had to move the statue a few feet, no one in my family was ever any the wiser. But God knew, from that day forward I'd make a terrible Franciscan.

Although not necessarily a terrible Catholic, and by no means a terrible priest.

Even priests were sinners in need of God's mercy and grace to be well. And, of course, if the Franciscans were the wrong fit, there were other orders I could join. What I'd been most taken with in those monks was never their communion with nature, never their love of all of creation's creeping things, but what I saw all holy people had in common, and what God asked of them: goodness and a sad loneliness.

Yet as much as I continued to identify with a priestly solitude, I was rarely sad in the ways that could be considered *religiously* sad. I rarely acted out the compassion, say, of visiting a widow. Even the widows I had at the ready—my grandmother, my mother's aunt Frances, or her cousin Margo—were generally more comforting to me than I was to them: fixing meals when my family visited, sending cards and checks on my birthday, telling me stories about my dad. They all seemed to be doing fine without their husbands.

And although terrified through the final years of the Cold War at the prospect of Russians launching nuclear missiles on nearby Chicago, I felt no awe, and suffered hardly any devastation at all, when faced with the violence of wars in Lebanon, Iraq, Bosnia, or Ghana. Wherever. Even at seventeen, I never watched the news. It was depressing and frightening, and I was sad and anxious enough. So focused on the beauty of my own soul, I was left with little room for what might have made me truly priestly or shaped a genuine calling.

Mired in a stranger sadness, I was the high school outcast who really loved it out on the fringes, crying the tears of a professional benchwarmer while always dreading my marching orders: "Korb, get in there! Play some defense!"

In my case, real popularity or any more playing time would have ruined everything. I delighted in getting called a queer.

It's not that I had the perspective then that has, over the past fifteen years, allowed me to see the great highs and seemingly greater lows of my teenage years in their proper light. (And never mind that fifteen more years may prove me wrong once again.) Forgetting an assignment in my hall locker would keep me up all night. Losing a tennis match could result in a McEnroe-style tantrum, a smashed racket, and a stern reprimand from my coach—the local Methodist youth-group leader—for muttering those curses under my breath. Every romantic crush that went nowhere broke my heart—each time irreparably. Neither did I believe my parents and those teachers who assured me that people like me—presumably the smart, ambitious ones who would inevitably leave this small town—would someday run the world. Ultimately I had very little interest in the world at all. That was what shaped my calling.

So I told them. "I think I should be a priest."

The news was hardly shocking, but as the words came out, one by one, they disappointed each of us. I could see it in their faces as they looked to each other for something to say. Despite the family lore that the mother of a Catholic priest, like the mother of God, was assured a place in heaven for all she'd done for the future of the church, my mom turned to me as if telling God, *No. I'm sorry. You can't have my boy. There's been some mistake.*

Realizing that my whole life was falling flat, I tried to take it back. I swallowed my words. "No, no," I continued, "It's God. It's God who thinks so." But already gone was their pride in the wise child. There had been some mistake. Gone was my wisdom. Suddenly none of us believed in me.

"But it's such a lonely life," my mother finally said. And my stepdad agreed.

My parents knew that in doing what I understood to be God's will for me, I would be making loneliness my profession and calling it a calling. They worried about me. And they were right to.

While it brings many men closer to God, the sacrament of holy orders would have certainly taken me away from him and led me into the sin of abandoning a world that is just sinful and imperfect enough to hate, if you let yourself. Rather than seeing this vocation as an opportunity to serve God through serving a congregation (and beyond)—the primary responsibility of Catholic priests—entering a seminary then would have been the greatest escape possible. The priesthood, as I saw it, offered me a lifelong hiding place. I could have forever stood apart from any pain, imperfection, and vulnerability—the worldliness of death, war, or even sex—doing nothing more than hating it and making a paradise out of my loneliness.

As much as I respect Ignatius and his order of devotees, the Jesuits, he was wrong. There is no medicine of immortality. Priestliness is not pharmacology. I was fooled. And we need only look again to John's Jesus for a sense of what's wrong with this kind of Catholic priestliness. In John, Jesus is the one who comes from above, and so is always above all.

Before his arrest on that eve of the Crucifixion, Jesus had already asserted his otherworldliness by turning the supper into a forum for a dying leader to deliver his last. In Jesus, the beautiful soul, "the absolute certainty of self thus finds itself," as Hegel put it, "converted directly into a dying sound." With all the abstract chatter and symbolic washing leading up to it, when Jesus finally gets around to serving up some food, it's impossible that the bread could be eaten at all. In John, everything Jesus touches becomes purely symbolic, and the apostles all go hungry. No one eats even the tiniest bit. And finally, following the Resurrection, where in the synoptic Gospels Jesus beckons and reassures his followers with "Do not be afraid," in John he remains aloof, practically scolding poor, frightened Mary Magdalene when she encounters him at the grave—*Noli me tangere!*—demanding that she not touch him, that he is not yet ascended to the Father, where he really belongs. Being one with God, Jesus can be the model of the perfect priest, someone who is apparently never hungry and, more important, someone who is perfectly alone on earth without ever experiencing loneliness. This model of priestliness is deathly, encouraging believers to turn their backs on this world and this life and to look only to the world to come. For its hatred of the world and its impossible demand that we preserve our beautiful souls and the certainty of the self, the priestly life that wooed me at seventeen threatens to take on the pallor of sin by separating us from God.

Perhaps knowing this, seeing this coloring to my face—although ultimately also still hoping for grandchildren someday—my parents tried to be kind. But the lonely life—the professional and holy solitude I'd always admired and found eternally comforting about the priesthood—had never seemed so empty. Without trying, my mother had again scolded me for speaking out of turn. They knew better than I did that this would be the worst form of quitting. Of hiding. Running away and escaping.

That's all it took from them. I was silent. I'd never been more scared. I wanted to cry.

So I went off to my room in a huff and let the fire die, realizing I'd have to make something of myself. On my own. Without God. In the world.

EPILOGUE
— PB —

When I first met Scott I had no idea he was such a prude. In fact, I thought he was one of the cool kids. I was always getting e-mails from him about parties and dinners, concerts and all-nighters. I never would have imagined him as a Catholic mama's boy tied to her apron by a rosary. And I certainly never would have imagined he ever wanted to be a priest. But as we got to know each other, it became clear that Scott's desire to be a priest was not just some scared teenager's desperate search for meaning. It was, and is, still an inherent part of who he is.

Over the years, as I watched him be a confidant—no less a father confessor—to his friends, myself included, I've witnessed how he renegotiates that young man's quashed desire. But in this priestly vocation there has also lain a quest for perfection, something that often revealed itself, at least to some extent, as unhealthy.

Scott has not taken any formal religious vows, but he's always been pretty good at being austere while also maintaining a certain hedonism. Scott walks in a world of excess, but he tries with all his might not to let it rub off on him. This is not so much priestly as it's vaguely monkish. Scott sometimes lives in a kind of monastery whose walls are constructed out of his desire for perfection—to protect this "beautiful soul." And in this way he still might be trying to have it both ways.

Scott abhors possessions. He rarely buys new clothes for himself, and when he does, they usually come from thrift stores. Every gift I've ever given him has been received with a strange mix of gratitude and aversion. He tells me he doesn't want things, doesn't want to get attached in any sentimental way to material items. We've argued about this, but never so fiercely as during debates about downloading music. Because Scott hates to purchase new things—and is probably a little cheap—he doesn't want to spend money on the frivolous acquisition of CDs. But he loves new music, is completely plugged into the independent music scene. So he copies his friends' CDs onto his computer. When I once insisted this was stealing, he worked out a complex moral justification. Since he goes to concerts of all these bands, he is giving them money they would not otherwise see if Scott hadn't heard the mp3s first. Go to the live show or buy the CD. No one can afford to do both. At once austere and hedonistic, he's amassed a huge collection of music without really having to own anything.

Nevertheless, priestliness itself is less about not participating in the material culture and more about being of service to friend and fellow. To be a priest is also less about celibacy than it is about ministering, less about vows to God and more about a promise to take care of the world. As it happens, this is where I always fall over myself. I want so much simply to be of service, without all the inner voices of reward and pride. Jewish philosopher Moses Maimonides organized levels of charity, from the most begrudging to the most selfless. Later commentary asks, "Which is the greatest of these?" The answer: They are all equal because the only one to whom any of this matters is the one who is receiving. The giver is simply a vessel. That said, I am still constantly weighing my actions against whatever outcome I perceive might result. It's more superstitious than faithful. I have seen Scott do the same in his own way. He, too, is sometimes afraid to not do the right thing. But while for him this serves his idea of perfection, I am sometimes weighed down by a strange and occult notion of good and bad.

Around the same age Scott conveyed his deepest wish to his parents, I conveyed a parallel, if not dissimilar one to mine. Unbeknownst to them at the time, I was knee-deep in a daily drug habit and getting deeper still. One night after a particularly vision-laden weekend, I felt I was on the cusp of something. The birds had been speaking to me, sending me messages, omens both foreboding and exciting. I knew enough to know this meant I might be crazy, but I also believed it might mean I was some kind of mystic, chosen for some greater spiritual journey. I decided to tell my parents. I decided to tell them I could hear the secret language of birds. They would be able to discern whether I belonged in a mental hospital or a monastery.

They were, of course, appropriately baffled and a bit shocked. And they did the best they could. Not really knowing about my then exceedingly well-hidden drug use, they urged me to think it through. My dad said, "But you know they aren't really speaking to you, right?" And so I decided to play along, realizing they couldn't help me. The truth of my mystical path was beyond even them. I assume they filed it away in the folder labeled Strange Teenage Phase, and we never spoke about it again.

What started as childhood wonder, a search for seeing God in all things, became a desperate paranoia. Like Scott, I once wanted to be something special for God: a spiritual warrior, a mystic. So I climbed, up and up and up. I went so high, tried to look at the sun straight on, and then fell and fell. God was there waiting for me, it turned out, exactly where I wasn't looking for him.

THE MYSTIC

— PB —

MY LUNGS WERE BURNING. My little wooden pipe had been cleaned and scraped so much that by this point I was smoking the pipe itself as I tried to get every last bit of resin trapped in the grain. I coughed up lungfuls of lighter fluid and air. I drank the last of my coffee brandy that I had mixed with a bit of vodka, but this only made me want to get stoned even more. In the corner of my room were bags full of garbage: beer cans, magazines, cigarette butts, and scraps of paper. I pulled out a newspaper from one of them and spread it out on the floor. Then I dumped a bag of garbage out and methodically picked through every piece of trash, looking for the accidentally discarded bud, the accidentally discarded roach. Enough of them and I could possibly get a small bowl of weed. My fingers darkened with ash and newspaper ink. The Syd Barrett record had finished and the needle was bouncing along the smooth inner circumference of the album. I was on my knees. I knew there was something in there somewhere.

I started the record over and went back to my task. Every time I listened to music I thought there was some message meant only for me hidden in the lyrics, but I could never quite understand what it was saying. It was decidedly worse with Syd Barrett than with Jimi Hendrix or the Beatles. I had latched on to him a year

THE FAITH BETWEEN US

earlier and listened to his records every night. I learned that he had gone crazy, fled from society, and lived in his mother's attic. Well, here I was in my parents' basement, and I wondered if I had access to the same knowledge that had destroyed him. I might be able to do it differently and be set free.

But I could never quite find what I was looking for. I never found the marijuana potent enough, never found the LSD pure enough. I knew that some secret knowledge, some magical formula for seeing God, was hidden somewhere in the world, but I was just not pure of heart enough, I thought. I was not intuitive enough. I was not enough of a spiritual warrior. I was too sick. I was evil. Or I was simply not high enough.

By this point, at twenty-one, I had stopped showering altogether. I had stopped brushing my teeth. Most days I was able to make it to work selling stereo equipment by throwing cold water on my face and putting on deodorant. I had to get through to get the paycheck to get the drink and the drugs.

I avoided my parents by sleeping until they left in the morning and coming home after they were asleep. The anxiety that drugs and alcohol had always relieved was back, now fueled by the drugs themselves. To smoke pot I had to get drunk first, or the paranoia and panic would be too much to bear. But even a few drinks made me feel crazy, so I had to try to get utterly wasted, to feel nothing. Along the way, I desperately tried to stave off thoughts of death. Everything around me became some kind of sign or symbol that I could not decipher but that ultimately represented my doom. And while I could not decode the secret messages hidden in the Syd Barrett record, I knew he was singing my funeral hymn. If you asked me what I thought I was doing, why things had gotten like this, I would have had no trouble telling you. I was looking for God.

The theologian Rudolf Otto has done a sort of natural history of the numinous, or what he calls the *mysterium tremendum*. In his slight yet important book *The Idea of the Holy*, Otto is interested in the nonrational aspects of religious experience, through which one encounters God, beyond ethical or dogmatic categories, as the "wholly other." Otto explains that our current usage of the word *holy*—something perfectly good—fails to invoke the origins of a word that once meant something majestic and terrifying, something "awful," as in inspiring awe, or awesome.

> The daemonic-divine object may appear to the mind an
> object of horror or dread, but at the same time it is no
> less something that allures with a potent charm, and the
> creature, who trembles before it, utterly cowed and cast
> down, has always at the same time the impulse to turn to it,
> nay, even to make it somehow his own.

In the development of religious thought, this "wholly other" starts to lose its more purely supernatural quality and eventually becomes an object of mystical devotion, utterly removed from phenomenal or worldly experience. In Jewish mysticism, the mystic often has to confront these terrifying aspects of God when encountering the *mysterium tremendum*.

Most religions have their mystical component, but in Judaism there is a whole varied cosmology, sometimes very different from the creation story in the Bible. Early Jewish mystics believed that the mystical knowledge was hidden inside the Bible, particularly the Torah, the first five books of the Hebrew scriptures. One of the most compelling and famous of these is the creation myth described in what is known as the Lurianic Kabbalah. In this story, first offered by Isaac Luria in the sixteenth century, before God could create the world he had to perform an act known as *tsim-tsum,* or contraction. A part of God needed to be emptied out before something new could be formed. Ultimately, however, this becomes an act of violence. What is emptied out still needs another vessel to contain it, and in Luria's conception, this God stuff cannot really be contained. The vessels shatter. As *creatures*—that which is created—our task is to restore the Godhead, in effect to undo creation so that God can be whole again. To be alive means to be apart from God. God is something so beyond our human experience, and yet we hunger for that union.

My home was a largely secular affair. My father, a sensitive rationalist, studied Hebrew via correspondence course in his spare time, and while he must have been reading the Bible, the substance of his studies never made it into our Passover seders. My mother, on the other hand, while also quite worldly, was privately and deeply spiritual. The manifestation of this in our home was her superstitions, which were often insistent and dogmatic. But she also prayed, sometimes alone, sometimes while she lit Friday-night candles. She often seemed sad in these moments, as if God were a lost or distant relative she missed, and she was telling him so. I walked between both of these religious identities, the rational and the emotional, over which Judaism hung like a wedding canopy. And within this—long before I'd read Otto or the kabbalah, long before I did any drugs—I sensed a glimmer of this God that is "wholly other."

As a child, I tried to induce states of altered perception in an effort to glean more fully this mystery. I tried to imagine where I went when I fell asleep, concentrating hard until I felt a sense of displacement. On some nights, lying in bed, I whispered, "I am me. I am me," until I felt a kind of vertigo. I experienced two identities simultaneously—I and me, one talking and one listening—both experiencing the same thing but stretching away from each other. The feeling was so exhilarating that I would have to hold on to the sides of the bed while waves crashed inside my belly. Eventually exhaustion would take me. Little did I know then that I would one day beg and steal in search of a similar kind of oblivion.

I was so afraid of these feelings, and yet what I wanted more than anything was to have control over them. Not to exorcise them or banish them, but to manipulate them, to find in the dread a kind of pleasure. I started to imagine that they had something to do with God, but I had no real religious training that would help me get at how or why. I began to believe that there was another reality one could have access to. I assumed the answers might be found in books.

In the library of Swampscott High School I had discovered the two small shelves that contained the school's collection of books under the Library of Congress card catalog subject heading "B-Philosophy, Psychology, Religion." There was an odd imbalance of books, which leaned heavily in the direction of popular sixties religious interests like Carlos Castaneda and Alan Watts. There was also in the library an ample supply of books on drug culture like Albert Hoffman's *LSD, My Problem Child* and the writings of Timothy Leary. Aldous Huxley's *Doors of Perception* read like a polite Victorian essay on what is the powerful hallucinogen psilocybin. These books were permission slips for excess and experimentation. Adults had written these books, which were in my school library and discussed the value of drugs and the possibility of liberation from all the suburban structures that had told me and my siblings, "*No!*" The mighty instrument of this liberation was drugs. And on the other side of this was not only mind expansion, but also a glimpse of the true nature of reality, a window to seeing God.

There is a great tradition of seeking God in excess. From the mystery cults of ancient Greece to certain Native American tribes who used peyote, many religious communities recognized the value of violent shifts in consciousness in helping to open the mind to the holy, to having a one-on-one with the gods. Author Daniel Pinchbeck calls this "breaking open the head." But we no longer have immediate access to the indigenous communities and the rituals that once made these experiences part of a larger religious system. The modern drug-induced spiritual experience, while often set communally, is still largely a subjective experience. Without teachers and shamans, our own desires usually get in the way. As Martin Buber might say, there is the danger that the experience would be nothing but an object of our own desires, not a way deeper into the holiness external to us.

Convinced that drugs were the window to see God, I was also determined to give my experiences some context in a tradition. I began to study religion, Eastern thought, the occult. I bought tarot cards and rolled the I Ching, the ancient Chinese oracle. I read about Aleister Crowley and other turn-of-the-century magicians to see if they had invoked something worth learning about. I looked everywhere but Judaism.

Being Jewish was simply the root of my home, the way we ate, the jokes I knew. But the God I wanted to know couldn't be there, I was certain. The God I wanted to know you didn't have to pray to. You experienced him. This is what I learned from people like Carlos Castaneda, who in the sixties went to Mexico as a student of anthropology in search of lore regarding medicinal plants. There he met the "sorcerer" Don Juan Matus, who after a series of tests allowed Castaneda to become his student. The driving forces behind Castaneda's first two books, mainly peyote and other herbal hallucinogens, were to propel him into the thick of the acid culture of the late sixties and early seventies. Not simply a catalog of trips, Castaneda's *The Teachings of Don Juan* describes a spiritual system that spoke to the religious longing of the time. This system contained a mix of Eastern and Western religious ideas like destroying preconceived notions of reality and the self, conquering fear, and gaining a kind of apolitical power that might one day be used to reshape the world. It is still not entirely clear what Castaneda was up to, how much of his writing was actually documentation of his experience, how much was exaggerated, and how much was simply fiction. For myself, Castaneda was like reading the greatest fantasy novel come true. I thought my friends and I played a decent game of Dungeons and Dragons, but here were real wizards, lycanthropes, and journeys to other dimensions.

What I took from Castaneda, as well as from Leary and Huxley, was that drugs were the key to opening a portal otherwise forever closed. Drugs were the bridge, really, between the desire for knowledge, to know God, and to experience other worlds, other realms—the levels of heaven, the circles of hell. There was more than twenty years of literature to justify this desire, to make the doing of it seem holy. (And to be honest, I just loved getting wasted.) So I started getting high all the time. Soon my first thought in the morning was how I would get drugs or alcohol that day. There was little in traditional morality, the morality of my family, that I was beholden to, since my goal was a lofty one: to see God. I could steal as long as I used the money for drugs. I could lie as long as lying was about protecting my lifestyle. (I could also lie in matters relating to sex, but at the time I couldn't quite figure out the spiritual justification.) I became expert in the kinds of drugs available, all the various types of marijuana, how to clean a pipe to get the resin, how to roll a joint two papers long and two papers wide. I knew the difference between Xanax and Valium and which worked better with alcohol. I knew how many beers to have before you lit up the bong for maximum effect. And while I got more and more stoned, I could never seem to get closer to God.

It wasn't until I took LSD that I witnessed all the wonderful and terrible aspects of that desire manifest in the chemical reaction of the drug. In one early instance, my friend Andrew had procured a few hits of blotter acid, a picture of a phoenix rising from a pool of flames adorning each tab on the sheet. The bird was skillfully detailed, its wings and beak gold and illuminated. The sheet seemed to vibrate as Andrew carefully tore off a hit for each of us.

Soon we found ourselves in the woods behind the golf course, part of the prestigious country club in our North Shore suburb. For a while I thought my hit was a dud. I felt a little stoned, but we had just finished a joint and it was impossible to tell what was what. Yet I was beginning to notice a peculiar kind of lucidity to my thinking.

We walked through the woods until we entered a small clearing. It was late October. The air was clean. The coolness of the day felt solid, but like gelatin, soft and easy to swallow. I felt a switch inside me click and suddenly the fallen leaves rose up and applauded me. They were covered in thousands of little V-shaped smiles that opened and shut as they rose and fell, the sound of their cheering like a balm. I had arrived at the place I had sought my whole life. For a time at least.

Over time my friends and I became connoisseurs, tasting the various kinds of acid as though they were fine wines. One of our favorites for a time was known as Pyramid, Cross, and Rose. The tabs were illustrated with a pyramid overlaid by a cross overlaid by a rose, the flower blossoming out of the center. Again, Andrew had gotten this acid. We invited a few other friends to the parking lot of a department store in a nearby town where Andrew had gotten a job picking up trash for five bucks an hour. We dropped the acid before we headed over to the lot, and it kicked in as we walked, halfway down the curving road. There was no sidewalk and we had to stay close to the edge, which was covered in a dense overgrowth of junk trees.

We walked single file, five of us in all, each starting to trip on either the pyramid, the cross, or the rose depending on our individual temperaments, it seemed, each component a different offering in our brains. I was torn between the three, feeling vaguely mystical, crucified, and organic all at the same time. Caught between the worlds this way was familiar, and I tried to find a groove. All the while my teeth were grinding. The acid was not so clean after all. We stopped at a construction site where an enormous crane sat with its neck lying on the ground, looking like a sleeping brontosaurus. We eventually made it to the parking lot, but cleaning the trash took forever, as each piece kept growing back, right out of the asphalt, as soon as we picked it up. Everything was humming. I could read my friends' minds. Every once in a while someone started laughing at a private joke, but someone else thought he got it and started laughing also. Then all of us were cracking up until a flash of how crazy it was made me panic and fall into a burrow of dark thought: Maybe we were like this trash we were picking up, ultimately abandoned by God, left to scatter in the wind.

As the years went on, I never really got any more seasoned with the drug. Each time was a crapshoot as far as how the trip would play out. I hoped I was opening a door to knowledge of God and the world, but all I really got was eight hours of trying to keep it together, along the way marveling at the trails of my moving hand, the physicality of sounds, the ringing in my ears that sounded like music—and trying to force the gloomier thoughts away.

Drugs are only the symptom of a deeper need that is, of course, far older than the psychedelic sixties. In fact, the desire to put a little mysticism back into the cultural consciousness was mostly a positive thing. But without religion and ritual, without story and symbol, sixties excess quickly degenerated into madness, crime, and the introduction of other kinds of drugs into the mainstream of American culture—cocaine, heroin, and speed, for example. The failure of the culture of drug-induced mysticism is that it offers the possibility of transcendence, but without structure or ethics.

Gradually the landscape of my mind, the environment where I existed, became more and more engraved with superstitious connections, paranoia. Getting high meant always having to come down, and I believed each time would be the one that would bring me to my heart's desire: union with God and liberation from the self, from my fears and anxieties. But eventually the drugs wore off and I was with myself again, lonely, bored, anxious, and needing to get high.

Somehow along the way I began to believe that the reason I was not able to experience God in any meaningful way was that there was something wrong with me. And the thing about the addicted mind is that it tells you that what you really need is more drugs. What might have at first helped lift the veil to offer a glimpse of transcendence became the very thing that prevented me from having any real connection with what I perceived as the holy. But the feeling of being high sure feels like transcendence, and so I kept on what was to prove an ouroborosian path.

I didn't know that mystics and kabbalists had been trying,

through a few thousand years of text and tradition, to make sense of the world in much the same way I was as they reached upward to God, climbing a ladder through the heavens toward a final mystical release. But these experiences are not freely given and traditionally require years of learning and religious exercises. The quick fixes offered by drugs and other new age spiritual prescriptions turn God into a spirit that haunts the world.

Nevertheless I kept looking for the right acid. I even tried something that had no image at all, just a little tab of washed-out brown. It didn't go very well. It was a Saturday in 1987, a year before I would finally get clean. I had dropped acid with my friends Michael and Valerie an hour before. The rain was making mud of everything. Even the asphalt had turned to liquid. Somehow we ended up on Boston's historic Charles Street, the rain falling so loudly we could barely hear each other. It felt as though it was only the three of us in the whole world. Under the eaves of a Laundromat we stopped to catch a glimpse of one another, soaking wet, laughing, maniacal. Something in me stirred. I suddenly felt how wet I was and thought it best to try and get dry. I had a mission, my own personal journey, apart from my friends. It was something I could call my own. Across the street was a diner that I frequented; it had the best turkey club in the city. I thought there might be something in there for me now. I looked at my friends and waved a short good-bye. They didn't see me. They were looking at each other as if gazing into heaven or the abyss. Who could know?

Michael, the son of a revivalist preacher, was a superhero to me. He could skateboard and Rollerblade; he had the best hash and even better marijuana. He was fearless, skating all over the city, in traffic, hollering and singing all the way. He had dismissed his father's evangelism but still considered himself a Christian. But he saw demons everywhere, much more than he saw angels. Valerie, on the other hand, was just a girl from the suburbs, yet she had a lightness and a simple wisdom that attracted us to her. They fell in love one afternoon while we were all getting stoned, and secretly I fell in love with both of them. We were just people who had met in the city, in a park. One of us was looking for weed and the other had it. Then, like many others, we formed an alliance. Trust. With one another we had a safe place to get drunk and stoned. A friendship blossomed out of the drunkenness.

In the diner I ordered tea, wiped off my glasses with a napkin, and sat at a table by the window so I could watch them. The tea and the warmth of the restaurant were a peace in my heart. I knew this place so well. I knew this street and knew my friends. I just wanted everything to be okay like this forever. I wanted the end of all desire. But desire was a ghost in the air no matter what, and my eyes needed something to fix on. I gazed down at my tea and then I noticed that the table was tilted. It rocked back and forth with the slightest pressure. Outside I could see Michael and Valerie. He was yelling at her, or so it appeared, his arms raised, moving in angry circles. She was just looking at him. I turned back to the table, to my cup of tea, to my dirty fingernails. I suddenly knew that things were *not* going to be okay. We could only take this so far. Eventually the whole life might come unraveled. We would all die. Why not tonight?

I was eighteen years old. I had been wearing the same clothes for going on three days. And we were all furiously tripping on two hits of unnamed brown blotter acid.

I left my tea and went outside, back into the rain, to see what was happening. I knew I was walking into the fray of something gone terribly awry, but how bad could it be? These were my friends. Michael saw me coming and pushed Valerie behind him.

Then he said, "I thought it was in her. I thought it was in her. But it was you all along. I cast it out! I cast it out!"

Valerie yelled, "Leave him alone!"

Something then seemed to pull him from his reverie. He turned, taking Valerie by the arm, and led her away from me, down Charles Street, into the rain. The exorcism was over just as quickly as it had started.

I fled. I ran to the subway station a few blocks away, my sneakers pressing deeper into the ground with each step. I could feel myself sinking. Under the sickly yellow light of the subway platform, I tried to pretend everything was cool. Then two young girls on the bench beside me threw me awful glances. I was translucent. I was exposed. I felt plastic, visible, fragile. I was coming undone. I ground my teeth to the seconds clicking down—waiting, waiting, waiting. And then a rumble, the behemoth of the subway rattling into the station.

I took the train to Park Street, then a serpentine Green Line train to Haymarket, where I waited for the bus to, please, take me home. I was either too early or too late for the bus, and the world became an old black-and-white TV that folds into a little white dot when you turn it off. It was either the devil, bad acid, or both, but whichever, my time was almost up. I knew that at least. And with whatever lucidity I had left, I picked up a laughing pay phone and dialed 911. A few minutes later—I could feel the rotation of the planet—two ambulances and a police car arrived. At this I thought, "I just needed someone to talk to."

Really, all we wanted that afternoon when we smoked the hash and dropped the acid was a glimpse of the ineffable, some proof of God in the only way we thought we could know God—to chew out of our own brains toward greater awareness. That was at three p.m. By ten o'clock I was strapped down on a gurney at the city hospital. I concluded in my delirium that God was not here, and if not here, then why anywhere? Funny, my bar mitzvah rabbi never told me about any of this.

At four a.m. my parents drove out from the suburbs to get me. I was crashing at this point, exhausted and confused. When my mother and father arrived, I was sitting in a room with a nurse. My parents looked miserable, old. The nurse suggested that I stay there and be put into a drug rehabilitation program. As far as my folks knew, this was a first, an experiment, an intellectual exercise just like Aldous Huxley had performed. I was their son, after all, not a drug addict, not a burnout. I didn't contradict them. I just wanted to get home so I could smoke the hash I had hidden in my shoe, and which the cops had failed to discover when they searched me, standard procedure for picking up a kid about to be hospitalized for a bad acid trip.

Despite my failure with acid, I continued to believe that without some dramatic experience, God would forever be something that eluded me. I refused, on principle, to believe that a real encounter with the holy could be had in the mundane workings of the actual world. Even without the drugs, the offerings of religious systems make it possible for any seeker to flit from spiritual lover to spiritual lover in a kind of religious promiscuity. While not an impossible way of encountering God, this path often doesn't offer the possibility of developing a disciplined and ultimately monogamous relationship with God. (And by monogamous I don't mean monotheistic. One can be a perfectly faithful pagan lover.) Jews seem particularly susceptible to this, dipping our feet into pool after pool of spiritual waters including Buddhism, all forms of Yoga, and even popularized versions of Jewish mysticism sans the Judaism. None of this is to say there aren't thousands of

perfectly enlightened Jewish Buddhists, but the sixties' appropria-
tion of Eastern spirituality in the West gave the next generation
easy access to what once required long treks to India.

One of the more interesting examples of this is in the story of
Ram Dass, born Richard Alpert (Jewish, of course). After getting
kicked out of Harvard along with Timothy Leary for their infamous LSD research, Alpert went off to India in search of the kind
of spiritual experience he had encountered on acid. The fleeting
nature of a hallucinogen will either make you easily forget it or
eagerly search for more, and so Alpert, having had a glimpse of
the spiritual in his LSD adventuring, went looking for other experiences. In India, Alpert met Maharajji Neem Karoli Baba, and in
what sounds like a vaguely apocryphal tale, Alpert gave Maharajji
LSD. After a few hours, Alpert noticed Maharajji didn't seem to
be responding. After more time passed, Alpert asked him what he
experienced. Maharajji said he had seen it all before.

Alpert stayed and studied and was eventually given the name
Ram Dass. Before he returned to America, Ram Dass asked Maharajji to tell him, finally, how to be enlightened, how to know
God. "Serve people. Feed people," is what his teacher told him.
Despite all the drugs, all the sex, all the music, all the demon-
strations, all the urgent desire for experience, the final answer
to the sixties quest for spiritual and physical liberation was, for
Ram Dass, "Serve people. Feed people." Nothing very subjective
there. And yet when he came back to the States, he was flocked
by hundreds of people and became one of the pivotal mouth-
pieces of Eastern spirituality in the West. Ram Dass brought both
the problem and the solution. He brought subjectivism in the
form of exotic spiritual nourishment, but that very nourishment was
a message of a simple objective ethic. The generation of seekers

that followed continued to stuff itself with the calories, but did not absorb much of the vitamins. Many people were still spiritually hungry.

By the time I was eighteen, having read almost everything on the two small shelves in the library and getting stoned, getting drunk, or tripping every day for two years, I was a nervous wreck. The desire to know God was no help to me at all. Getting high and drinking had become my primary objective. Over those years, I constantly felt that I was about to fall apart, and that drugs were the glue. Slowly my thinking began to change, to shift, so that straight or stoned, there was no distinction. Getting high sharpened my focus, or so I thought, and relaxed me long enough to read and listen to music. When I wasn't high I was trying to get high, so the anxiety of getting money together, calling the dealer, looking for a buyer, standing around—and the waiting, waiting, so much waiting—ate away at me. And all the while I wanted to encounter some aspect of the divine, of the sacred. How ancient was this desire—if I had only known there was language and ritual for it. But it wouldn't have stopped me. Drugs were a moral bomb shelter. There was neither good nor evil in procuring and taking them. Drugs were impervious to conventions of civility and ethics. Steal, lie, cheat, beg, borrow, plead. The world was all an illusion anyway, true reality a pulsing, shifting language under the surface, a text of symbols and signs that could be read if conditions were just right, if you had the right combination of drugs.

Eventually getting high became chemistry and algebra in a quest to solve a particular spiritual equation: one part LSD, two parts Valium, a six-pack of beer. Scratch. Two parts LSD, one gram of black hash, a bottle of whiskey. Scratch. First the beer, then add acid, save the pot for coming down eight hours later. Scratch. Open mouth and pour it all in, come what may.

As many who have survived to tell about it say, the most drugs can ever offer is a glimpse—and even that is faulty, a vision made up of ego and desire. Carlos Castaneda wrote that he later discovered that Don Juan was hesitant to give him mescaline at all, and that it was used simply as a kind of bludgeon to get Castaneda to open his mind.

According to Simone Weil, we cannot experience God in any perfect way, since in our finite state we cannot traverse the infinite distance to God. This was how drugs lied to me, by continuing to promise that if I kept using, I could make that journey. Weil did believe that although we can never perfectly know God, if someone is suffering in a particular way, we can experience a perfect separation from God. Weil called this state "affliction" and believed it to be a state of perfection:

> Affliction is a marvel of divine technique. It is a simple and ingenious device which introduces into the soul of a finite creature the immensity of force, blind, brutal, and cold. The infinite distance separating God from the creature is entirely concentrated into one point to pierce the soul at its center.

It is in this experience of the "perfect absence of God" that God may make himself known. For Weil, only God can make the journey toward us. Only God can cross the infinite, our suffering a perfect path. My own affliction revealed the absence of God to me as well, but I realized something slightly different. God might make the journey toward me, but I was going to have to make some effort to meet him halfway. No one had told me this before. Religious people I had met thought that simply by saying the words and following the law, one would slowly be transformed: Believe, and experience will come. Timothy Leary and others like him insisted that you had to totally transform yourself first, destroying consciousness along the way, and then the reality of God would be revealed.

In all the previous years, in all the searching, in all that I read, in all the visions, both beautiful and terrible, in all the sex, friendships, arguments, in every acid trip and every pipe, in every bottle, in every song and in every album, in every place I sought God, I never once thought to look for God by simply asking God. But one day in June 1988, after a night of hallucinations and vomiting, I woke up knowing that one more time and I would be dead. For real. Never mind the devils and demons I thought were coming to kidnap my soul. Whatever my spiritual condition, I was at the end of my physical life.

I knew someone who had stopped drinking years before, and not knowing what else to do, knowing I didn't dare drink or get high again, I called him.

"You need to ask for help," he said.

"Help me."

"Not me. You need to ask God for help."

It felt like he slapped me. It undermined everything I had ever believed. It meant that God was not an equation to be solved, an experience to be had, but a place to go to. It meant that I could act, that I had some power left, if only enough finally to surrender. And once I gave up that final bit of power, then maybe something would change. So I did it. I flushed the last of my drugs down the toilet and I asked God for help. It was not the god of Castaneda. It was not the god of Leary. It was simply a god that was not the emptiness inside me, not the anxiety coursing through my blood. It was simply a god that I had never once thought to pray to in any way. It wasn't the god I learned about during my bar mitzvah training. But in a way, it felt like the god my mother prayed to on Friday nights, an old acquaintance lost to time. I was not sure if this god would answer if I called on him. But for one minute I believed that he might hear me. So I got on my knees and I said, "God help me."

And I didn't get high that day. Or the next. Or the next. Or the next.

During the first few years of being clean, I decided that anything that looked in any way like mysticism was a danger to me. It was a road that would only lead me back to drugs. I couldn't separate the two things, and so believed that I had to abandon any hope that I could have an encounter with God as Otto's *mysterium tremendum*. I would never witness God as anything other than the simple fact of my sobriety. God was saying to me what he had said to Moses, that I would die if I tried to see his face. I started to take on a little religious practice, but it was all surface experience. Religion was the ice that I skated on, and God was the death that awaited me in the cold depths below. So I stayed along the thicker edges, every once in a while trying to get closer to the thinner middle where I thought I could peer through the ice and catch some glimpse. But I was so afraid. What I wanted was something I was not allowed to have. In my search for God, for some kind of experience, I had forgotten the ethical and the moral. I had become a liar and a cheat, a thief and a deceiver. I had stolen the money I needed to get high and justified it by calling it a spiritual quest. And so this way was barred to me. I would only get to know God in the most superficial way.

But then something happened that I didn't expect. I didn't

expect it at all. I discovered that all along God had been in the place I had never thought to look for him. God was in the world. The prayer known as Adon Olam expresses this resolution. The first part of the prayer describes the God of the mystics, the wholly other, the ineffable God I once ached to experience:

> *Master of the Universe, Who reigned*
> *Before any form was created,*
> *At the time when His will brought all into being,*
> *Then was His Name proclaimed.*
> *After all has ceased to be,*
> *He, the Awesome One, will reign alone.*
> *It is He Who was, He Who is,*
> *And He Who shall be in splendor.*
> *He is One—there is no second,*
> *To declare as His equal.*
> *Without beginning, without conclusion.*
> *He is the power and dominion . . .*

This is the God I feel intuitively. This is, no doubt, a God who is. This is the God I believe in, but it's a God that I cannot be in relation with, a God I cannot know. Terrible, wonderful, the destroyer and the creator.

The second half of Adon Olam says something very different about God than the first half, in which God is alone, unknowable, eternal, forever, with or without us. The prayer takes an abrupt turn and each line slowly moves into the world from that which cannot be known to that which is the most familiar:

> *He is my God, my living Redeemer,*
> *Rock of my pain in time of distress.*

He is my banner, and refuge for me,
The portion in my cup on the day I call.
Into His hand I shall entrust my spirit
When I go to sleep—and I shall awaken!
With my spirit shall my body remain,
Hashem is with me, I shall not fear.

As you move through the lines, the language and images become more and more intimate and personal—rock, banner, cup, hand, sleep, spirit—until we are at last with God, and we shall not fear. It is a catalog of metaphors, each one a distillation of what cannot be spoken of in the first place. It seems to say: Whoever this God is for you, make it a God of the world. But remember: Never forget the first half of this prayer, where the God that forms from formlessness will one day take you from this world, and then one day will take the whole world as well.

I sometimes still want God to burn me up, to set my face on fire, but I am more afraid of that God now. Fear of God is almost cliché, but the idea can have so many different connotations. In the same prayer we are often asked not to fear death but to fear God. Psalm 112 reads, "Praiseworthy is the person who fears God . . . their heart is steadfast, they shall not fear." There is also a wonderful Hasidic tale about a rabbi who loved God but was not afraid of God. So he prayed for the fear of God. God answered his prayers and drove the rabbi to his knees. He called out, "Please, God, take away this fear!" There is also a tension with the kind of fear that is often expressed in religious language. There is fear that is more like awe, and fear that is more like dread. The latter often drives you away from God; the former is rarely found. In Genesis, when Jacob sees the angels ascending and descending the ladder, he exclaims,

"How awful is this place." Not "Man, this God business is terrific stuff," but rather, "Holy shit!"

When I encounter God in the world—seeing a remarkable bird, making love to my wife, witnessing my son in deep play—I often feel something in my soul tremble. Sometimes I feel the same when I encounter the absence of God—in images of war, terrorism, human brutality. And in all these instances I remember to be afraid. But then I try to remember that God is my rock, who freed me from the bondage of drugs, from the bondage of seeking God in only one way, who taught me that a desire for the biggest mystical experience was really the most limited of all.

EPILOGUE
— SK —

Although I've been stoned exactly twice, both times in my late twenties, I've always loved drug stories. My only actual encounter with cocaine—also in my late twenties—came when my lips went numb after kissing a girlfriend who'd done a quick line before I'd arrived for a date; even that inspired a brief panic that I might die. There's no such risk in just hearing a story, though. So through Peter I maintain my own vicarious addiction, the only kind possible for a lifelong control freak. And he's told me everything.

Only a few weeks clean, Peter prepared to move into a big, old house in Lynn, just eleven miles north of Boston along the coast, and the next town over from Swampscott, where, in high school, he first fingered the spines of those books by Carlos Castaneda and Aldous Huxley. A friend had offered the place after Peter approached him desperate for a better living situation than with his

crack cocaine–addicted housemate. Going from one place in Lynn
to another with hardly any possessions to speak of—he'd only recently sold the last of his comics collection for $250—was by no
means a big move, but it was an important one. After several false
starts and all those years of unholy hallucinations, this must have
seemed like a first real move toward God.

The house was undergoing renovations, so when Peter arrived
it stood completely empty. *What a relief!* God had helped him.
God had brought him here to a new home. He would be safe. He
could have a fresh start. God would be waiting inside. Maybe he
could even learn to pray to him.

But something was wrong. Still more or less addled, Peter's
mind worked overtime those days, not just on staying clean, but
also on controlling the religious superstition he'd inherited from
his mother, which all those drugs had regularly transformed into
full-blown paranoia.

Although still focused on finding, and now thanking, God, the
fearful possibility of actually encountering the divine still overwhelmed Peter, threatening him with the same oblivion he'd found
in blotter acid. The memory of his friend Michael's ad hoc Christian exorcism, which had left Peter trembling with the fear of God,
was also relatively fresh. So I imagine that same childhood panic
swept over him, crashing in his belly, when, after dropping his
bags and making a first tour of the house, he discovered God waiting there for him. A vision of Jesus dangled at the end of a discarded rosary hanging from a doorknob.

Someone was playing a cosmic—and in the moment, it must
have seemed cataclysmic—practical joke. If this was the sort of
help God had to offer, a haunted house and another inscrutable
sign, Peter wasn't sure he needed it. He wasn't sure he could handle it.

As for the rosary itself, he wasn't sure what to do with it. So, in no condition then even to try deciphering what God had meant in leaving it there for him—and surely God had meant *something*— Peter simply kept it. If it came from God, he had no other choice. He found a place for it in his drawer. He took it with him when he moved away from Lynn. As he took his first modest steps back toward Judaism and really learned to pray, he still held on to the beads. He married Amy, his mother died, and his son was born; he moved again, and again—and all the while, the rosary followed.

Suffice it to say, my own drug experiences were by no means religious ones. No leaves ever rose up to applaud me. No son of any revivalist preacher ever performed a rain-soaked, delirious exorcism to expel my demons. There was no trip. There was no fall. I would never have let such a thing happen to me. God did not exist in some mystical void; God could not be hallucinated.

No, if God was to be found anywhere, it was in the very things that had escaped Peter—the things that he'd absolutely eschewed— during all those years of hopeless searching. Because, as a Catholic, I'd always had what Peter needed: fixed language and ritual. Basically that was all I'd ever had.

As rosaries go, the one that haunted Peter for all those years is nothing special. Made in Italy, it may be Vatican issue, but I doubt it. The beads are cheap, brown plastic, and although the chain itself is metal, the whole thing weighs almost nothing at all. The Holy Mother, the object of devotion when Catholics count the fifteen decades (or tens) of Hail Marys, often hoping for her intercession with God, is stamped lightly on the centerpiece where the beads branch into a necklace. And below that, a pathetic, faceless Jesus is nailed to a tiny, imperfect wooden cross. All the rosaries I've ever owned—and growing up, I had several hanging from my headboard, most of which I've kept over the years—have been more substantial than this one, with brighter and smoother beads that make a much more pleasing sound when they come together in my hand. Much less pathetic, the other crucified Christs really seem to suffer.

Of all the drug-related stories Peter has told me, my favorite, and the one I've asked to hear again and again, is the one about that house in Lynn. Not so long after we met, just after we'd each admitted a belief in God, he included the story in a letter he mailed along with the rosary. And through that letter, I learned all about the early days of his recovery long before I knew all of what he had recovered from. I've known from the very beginning that his addiction was a spiritual crisis as much as a physical one; his recovery as much a path to what he would call an authentic relationship with God as a way to health of mind and body. And the spiritual recovery took far longer.

Peter was clean for more than a decade before he could give up that rosary, before he could stop clutching it from apartment to apartment, before he could admit that, despite all his past worries and near paralyzing superstition, for him and his faith, those beads actually mean nothing at all. The wrong God had not been haunting that house in Lynn.

And despite the fact that I received the rosary during a time when my own faith in the actual power of fixed language and ritual was on the wane—just after the attacks of September 11, more than a year after my stepfather retired, complaining that he was just so tired all the time, and some months before he died—Peter's beads are still meaningful for me. Most rosaries just aren't.

See, after the attacks, when love and near-constant companionship was my only comfort in the face of my greatest fears, I might have stopped believing in the rosary's power over sin and death.

But Peter's actually proved it. Just as with all those other rosaries I've been carrying with me all these years, there's no magic in this one. And when he no longer needed it, when his faith in God was strong enough, Peter gave it away. Finding this true faith in God—a recovery over not just drugs, but actually over real sin and death—is the miracle of Peter's rosary, and as I've learned, this is the only kind of miracle worth believing in.

THE VIRGIN

— *SK* —

OF COURSE, IT WASN'T JUST THE SEX that was bringing us together every night. From what I could tell, since the attacks not even the most fearless loner was sleeping alone. Given the choice in normal circumstances, people seem to prefer company through the night than to spend it by themselves; and faced with the unprecedented unnormalness of all that death, and all so close, a good night's sleep seemed impossible without someone there to assure you that you'd make it till morning. My girlfriend, Jane, assured me.

Prayers were no use. Despite every claim to the contrary, God had nothing to do with what had happened. He had no answers. Prayers for the martyred terrorists were canceled out by prayers for the martyrs trapped in the buildings. And, as Jonathan Franzen observed in the *New Yorker* on September 24, 2001, "On the street, after the impact, survivors spoke of being delivered from death by God's guidance and grace."

You know there's a problem with God when terrorists, victims, and survivors all hold an equal share.

No one was arguing with Franzen, though, when he continued, ". . . even they, the survivors, were stumbling out of the smoke into a different world." And for those like me who might normally

107

have turned to God—America was full of them, "in many cases, praying to their God for a diametrically opposed outcome"—the old words no longer held any promise. The Psalms were suddenly wrong. God was not like a fortress; he was not like a shepherd. The prayers from the Gospels had always promised comfort and protection by God, who was like a father. At this point, though, it seemed more appropriate to pray Jesus' dying and blasphemous complaint from the cross: *Eloi, Eloi, lema sabachthani!*—My God, my God, why have you forsaken me! Even the Koran's habit of describing Allah only in terms of what he is *not*—*e-ternal, un-begotten, ab-solute*—seemed like a bad idea. Here we were again, reckoning not just with the problem of how an absolute God could allow such terror, but worse, how he could be the inspiration for what Franzen was calling the "death artists." For Richard Powers, like Franzen a writer assigned by a New York publication to make some sense of the rubble in the days after the impact, "The always-thereness of here was gone . . . No comparison can say what happened to us." Yet where Franzen's reflection looked ahead to the days when we could again "awaken to our small humanities," Powers, writing from Illinois for the *Times Magazine*, seemed to want more—and *now*, with the nation still facing the rubble: "But we can start with the ruins of our similes, and let 'like' move us toward something larger, some understanding of what 'is.'"

And in those days, when the only thing worse than the fear was being alone with the fear, what "is" was Jane. There was no comparison necessary, or even possible, and no *small* humanity in her.

Over the years since moving to New York I've kept a meticulous calendar in a small, old three-ring binder. At the top of each page I scrawl the date in blue capital letters. Under that I keep lists of things to do, places to be, and people to call or write. Every few months I refill this book and collect the stacks of used pages in a desk drawer as a kind of diary, my own little record of "the always-thereness of here."

By my records, Jane and I met FRI 27 JULY–PARTY. Earlier in the evening I'd apparently had HAPPY HOUR. 6P.–BALCONY, and, since I'd crossed it off, I'd probably also watched a movie in my living room, after having grilled FOOD, ETC. with friends. After being introduced that night, Jane and I danced at the party, she took me home, and we sat on the balcony outside my bedroom, the grill perhaps still warm, sharing a glass of wine—all that was left after HAPPY HOUR. We sat until dawn when she drove away with my number. I hesitated that night to explain what her roommate Beth, who had invited both of us to the party, had meant when she warned Jane that I was "pretty religious."

Over the next month—following a first date, leading up to which I wondered in my calendar WHAT TO DO? —Jane and I did all this at least:

> PORT AUTHORITY BOWLING.
>
> CONEY ISLAND.
>
> DINNER–CALL.
>
> WHITE STRIPES–PIER 54–HUDSON RIVER PARK.
>
> ASTORIA.
>
> PERFORMANCE.
>
> HAPPY HOUR.
>
> PICNIC–AFTER 5P.
>
> BONNIE PRINCE BILLY–WLMSBRG.

We hardly slept during those first weeks of our relationship, often taking long rides in the middle of the night with her on the back of a bike. Midweek she'd wake up for me if I rang her bell at four a.m. after studying late, then we'd talk for a few minutes, meddle with each other under the sheets, and then drift off. We'd fool around in the mornings, too, before I went to class and she rode off to work a waitress job at Central Park's Tavern on the Green, taking the bike we shared.

For the first time in my life I had someone with me all the time, someone always to think about. I'd dated, but no one had ever felt this much like a partner. And it was this young partnership that made us feel so alive, that life was better when you shared it with someone. It was something I'd quietly envied about Peter and Amy ever since his first letter to me, which described Amy's sleeping habits while pregnant with Sam, recounted a household disaster with a drain trap, and told how together husband and wife, Peter's royal "we," were working to keep his cholesterol down. That early letter had said it all: Living had not been as good without someone else worrying about his heart.

Jane's roommate Beth had known me as a seminarian. She knew I went to church. That I had always gone, every week, sometimes every day. I prayed. She knew I taught religious education classes. I'd grown up Catholic. I'd wanted to be a priest. So it's clear, in any context, that I might have been considered pretty religious. But when Beth disclaimed the introduction she'd arranged between the two of us by issuing Jane that particular warning while I went off collecting beers for everyone from the crisper, she meant something pretty specific: *Jane, you should know, he's not going to have sex with you.*

Virginity, though, was a technicality. It always had been.

Though I never got "the Talk," my early religious life was full of talk about sex. Treated in my family with equal parts silence and shame, sex quickly became, like other pleasures I knew to cause proper guilt, an entirely religious matter. And it should come as no surprise that religious virgins (even the virgin-in-training I was as a very young boy), seemingly more than anyone else, become obsessed with the constant threat and temptation of sex. As with soldiers being trained for war—a common point of comparison for today's virgins fighting the good fight against sex and the world, those allied enemies in "every man's battle"—the more you prepare, the longer you'll live. And the Christian hope is, of course, to live forever.

The church stumbled all over itself to show me its deep love for virgins, even giving us holy days that celebrated a sex-free life. On these days, which were rarely Sundays, we had to go to church, usually after dinner. And before I stopped confusing it with the Christian myth surrounding the Annunciation, I understood the Feast of the Immaculate Conception as honoring the perfect, magical way to make a baby, better than any fantasy stork, and without the pain and mess I would before long come to associate with physical intimacy: Mary became pregnant with the Son of God while maintaining her virginity. This is not, however, what is meant by the Immaculate Conception. And to clear up the confusion that still affects even most Catholics I know: It is Mary, and not Jesus, who is honored for being Immaculately Conceived. Mary's mother, Anna, and her father, Joachim, did have sex; the miracle of her conception is that, unlike for the rest of us, Mary's did not involve the stain of original sin. Again, the Annunciation, a different holy day entirely, celebrates the miraculous conception of Jesus, the moment when the angel Gabriel comes from on high to ask Mary if she would carry the Son of God, and she agrees: "Be it unto me according to thy word."

And finally, as a young Catholic becoming more and more preoccupied with sex as each new concept was introduced during church (*virginity, celibacy, conception*), there was also the matter of

Mary Magdalene, the famous New Testament prostitute—another term to be wrapped in euphemism: woman of the night, of ill repute, of easy virtue—and the perfect, *fallen* love interest for Jesus. Yet in the Gospel of John, where Jesus states most clearly that the believer must hate the world, he preserves his chastity as the model of difficult virtue, even after the Resurrection, and seems to scold her: Do not hold on to me; don't touch me, he says—*Noli me tangere!* And so she stays away. She lets go. For my part, confused between Holy Days of Obligation and terrified of someday being scolded by Jesus if I hadn't abstained or been disciplined enough— if I hadn't in essence turned my back on many of the pleasures and promises of living—it's no wonder I was terrified of sex.

Where God was concerned, sex was for married people, not for me, and also somehow associated with dying (or not): "Sexuality," the catechism reads, "by means of which man and woman give themselves to one another through the acts which are proper and exclusive to spouses, is not something simply biological, but concerns the innermost being of the human person as such. It is realized in a truly human way only if it is an integral part of the love by which a man and woman commit themselves totally to one another until death."

The best examples of man and woman we had from the Bible, though, were Jesus and his mother, neither of whom ever committed themselves totally to another person, and neither of whom, ultimately, would ever actually die. For her part, Mary was not just *a* virgin but *the* Virgin, a title bestowed for being *ever*-virgin. And as the mother of God and totally unstained by the world, tradition had it that she was one of two people ever taken bodily into heaven; the other was, of course, her undying, resurrected son, another *ever*-virgin. Both received the perfect, deathless reward for leading perfectly ascetic, sex-free lives.

Like every Christian I'd ever known, I wanted a reward as close
to this as possible. I assumed their discipline and their aloofness. If
I had to die someday—and as a boy, even one whose father had
died, I'm not sure I believed I would, necessarily—eternal life in
paradise was the perfect promise, and in a sense the very thing I
lived for. Who would ever risk losing heaven for a sinful little roll
in the hay?

I began really not having sex at fourteen, when sex first became a
possibility and I finally got touched. The summer before I started
high school my mother drove me to my girlfriend's farmhouse at
least three times a week. Lynn's young mother sat chain-smoking
in the kitchen, or busied herself in the barn feeding horses and a
goat, or wandered to the basement with the laundry. Lynn led me
upstairs by the hand, where, after I removed the plastic retainer
keeping my teeth straight—she still had braces—we fell immediately to long afternoons of awkward, impatient groping. Lynn
was taller than me, more attractive, had dated a boy already in
high school; she brought to her bedroom floor both three months
more experience than I had and a euphemism for everything. I
shot a hand up her shirt. A few weeks into June she began removing her tiny bra before I even arrived; I learned not to wear a belt,
making it easier for her to jab a dry hand into my shorts. Imitating
what sexiness I had learned from movies, I undid the button of her
jeans and, having no idea what to do, with my free hand in her
pants I left a lot to be desired, she said.

And so from the very beginning virginity was a technicality.
The grave sexual sin was intercourse. Hand jobs on the floor were
okay, even while over time they became more of a pain than a
pleasure. A hand job in Lynn's waterbed, however, was not okay,
and one afternoon, when we were left completely alone in the

THE FAITH BETWEEN US

house, I made us scramble back to the floor where it was safe, where I could not accidentally, by the force of a wave, fall into having sex with her.

In ninth grade we talked about getting married one day, and, more important for her, about strolling through a trellis into our junior prom, dancing close, and later leaving together; all that year I lied to her when I agreed that we'd lose our virginity with the rest of our class that night, in a hotel room, in a car, in my parents' house, or on that waterbed. "Prom" was, for me, the best euphemism ever, safe, more than two long years away. And at the end of the school year, when she kissed another boy, I was relieved we could finally break up.

After that I got so I could practically masturbate in my sleep. This, like the hand job, was a sin by Catholic standards, and was accompanied by standard Catholic guilt. So each time I promised myself, and God, I'd never do it again. But these promises, it seemed, were made to be broken. And as sins went, premarital sex was just far worse—unforgivable, to my imagination, a permanent blemish on my soul. Once lost, virginity was not something you could get back. I needed the technicality. The sacrament of confession or, short of that, my simple silent prayer for forgiveness—those broken promises never to touch myself again—would repair damage done to a dirty, lying conscience, but there were different consequences where sex was involved. The catechism was clear: Sex outside of marriage is adultery, a mortal sin that "destroys the charity in the heart of man by a grave violation of God's law; it turns man away from God, who is his ultimate end and his beatitude, by preferring an inferior good to him." Not only that, but sex led to pregnancy and abortions— shameful and sinful in themselves—and all sorts of other troubles that were too much for a kid to deal with.

I had gotten an early start, and dating in high school was always more of the same: talks on the phone and hand jobs on floors. When I started college, beds became fine for making out, but falling asleep together at some degree of nakedness threatened my modesty. Either she or I walked home late at night, crossing the campus at the University of Wisconsin, where winters are punishing. On one occasion, I prepared the couch for a girlfriend who lived out of town—too far to walk—and she slept in the living room, where my roommates found her in the morning before I even woke up.

Until I met Jane, my life in New York had hardly been any different. I'd finally become comfortable sharing a bed, although it had become harder to explain the no-sex rule with each passing year. One girlfriend once tried to convince me that if I really liked her I'd have sex with her. Needless to say, I didn't like her enough. I couldn't have. So we broke up. In other relationships, I came up with lame excuses, or no excuses at all, to end them.

Beth was, of course, right. "Pretty religious" was probably even an understatement.

Virgins, I believed, could live above the fray, an enviable position, unsullied and free from certain complications, dangers, and sorrows of living in the world. They don't get scolded; there's nothing to fear. They avoid most threats of sexually transmitted diseases and so stave off death in one of its many forms. They're carefree of unwanted or unprepared-for pregnancies and, of course, the question of abortion never becomes a truly personal matter. Not to mention that sex can make for messier emotional entanglements than those activities that for most everyone in his twenties and thirties are considered foreplay, but for me had always been the bona fide play, all she could hope for: from a first hopeful peck to fumbling around with a vibrator, my hands all over her while she struggled with my pants. Still proud of a lost vocation to the priesthood, scared of sex, and scared of the sorrows of the world, I'd long ago taken the Catholic vow of celibacy.

I'd been proud to be a virgin. Scared not to be.

But I knew I wouldn't want to die that way.

Soon after we met, Jane and I signed up as cohosts for a weekly late-night show at WBAR—Barnard College radio. My enrollment in Columbia University's PhD program and a mandatory orientation qualified us to play indie rock albums on-air at the neighboring women's college. We called our show "All My Daydreams Are Disasters," after a line from a favorite country song. Tuesday night, September 11, 2001, would have been just our second appearance.

We never made it, though, and we weren't alone in missing our shift. As far as I know, beginning around half past nine that morning, when it became clear to everyone that the crashes downtown were no accident, our frequency remained silent all day. And with neither a wire service nor a broadcaster on staff capable of comprehending what was happening, much less reporting it, this student-run station was not really able to be in the business of delivering the news.

For some, it was the fear of death that shut the station down. For others, it may have been respect for the dead. New York had become one big funeral. Early estimates were upward of five thousand lost and buried. Who could play rock music when we needed a dirge? Unlike most media outlets in the city, our station did not rise to the occasion. For my part, I wanted us as far away from Manhattan as we could get. So Jane and I slinked away over the bridge by midafternoon—many hours before our show was supposed to start—and disappeared with a crowd into the outer borough of Queens, where Jane lived.

I share a birthday with the Holy Mother, September 8, nine months after the Feast of the Immaculate Conception, and that year three days before the disaster. Looking back over my calendar cum diary, there was a PARTY planned for my twenty-fifth birthday. We packed my apartment, even emptying out my bedroom to make space for the overflow-smokers who had to stand on the balcony. Jane came, met my friends, and stayed the night. After the apartment emptied out around three a.m., she and I carried my mattress back from my roommate's bedroom and slept a foot off the floor Saturday and Sunday. For many of my guests, the cab ride home from my party over the Brooklyn Bridge and up the West Side Highway early Sunday morning was the last they ever saw of the World Trade Center.

The night before the attacks, Monday, September 10, I stayed in Queens. Facing an early class in the morning, I sneaked out of Jane's house before either of us was fully awake. I boarded the M60 bus into the city while the sky was still nearly white, probably two hours before it became among the brightest, clearest, and most glorious late-summer days New York had ever seen. The school year had just started and I was already unprepared for my lectures. Jane was making it hard to keep up with the reading. So I sat nervous and impatient through my morning lecture, avoiding eye contact with the professor, writing in the margins even though I was a hundred pages behind—and unbeknownst to me, or anyone else in the room, about ten miles from danger.

Having planned to meet after class that morning at a café near Columbia, Jane and I were together just after the attacks, hours before we'd see any footage or learn that the Pentagon and a field in Pennsylvania were also on fire. Above us sounded the steady mourning bells of the Cathedral of St. John the Divine, already telling Harlem, Morningside Heights, and the Upper West Side that something had happened downtown, entirely out of sight.

We reached our families and left messages for friends from the phone in the basement kitchen of Corpus Christi Church. I had been going there since my first Sunday in the city, teaching religious education in the school gymnasium every Saturday. The priest Ray Rafferty had become a good friend. When I rang at the rectory door, he poked his head out, waved us in, and showed us downstairs. "The south tower collapsed," he said. "It's gone."

After speaking with our parents from the basement, Jane and I left the church, and while sitting in the courtyard of my old home, Union Seminary, off the street to find what seemed calm, we overheard that the north tower went.

So we fled. For hours, though, as Jane and I wandered the neighborhoods heading east toward the river to get out of the city, I imagined terrorists poised in the open doors of vans mowing down pedestrians with guns. We became part of the endless emptying of Manhattan Island, our eyes drawn back to the great damage done hours earlier as we dragged each other arm in arm across the roadway of the Queensboro Bridge. A long black smudge in the skyline made its way over the river into Brooklyn.

And marching forward, averting our eyes, all I could think about was her bedroom. Her mattress on the floor. All we wanted was each other and some quiet. The bridge was overrun. The walk was long. We reached Queens by three and caught a jammed bus partway to the apartment.

Still in our clothes, we collapsed into what had become by now a loving and familiar sexless tangle of limbs, twisted and sweat-dampened sheets, and her cool white comforter; with music quiet on the stereo, and wanting each other, we slept instead through the late afternoon with her shades drawn on that ruined day. At first when we woke again neither of us believed the day could still be ruined. It was still so beautiful. We were disoriented by a second morning to the day, by again having to rub our eyes and yawn at the same white light outside.

Just before seven that evening we took her car to find some television news at a friend's house midway between her apartment and mine in South Brooklyn. Beth, the woman who had introduced us, was there too. Safe. And finally, still later, passing through a spotlit police barricade with a utility bill as evidence that, *Yes, I live this way down that street, officer,* we arrived at my house just as our radio show would have been wrapping up another Tuesday, bleeding into Wednesday. A thin layer of ash coated the cars and the plaster Virgins and Holy Families in front of the houses down my block, the fig tree and my Italian landlord's perfect hedges. The windows had been closed too late to keep the place from reeking of sour smoke. Like death. It would smell that way for weeks. Most of the city did.

Though the house was quiet, it was impossible to sleep. Yet we lay mostly still that night, out of consideration for the other, touching as always but not wanting to move for fear that by some miracle one of us had actually drifted off and even the brush of a naked back would ruin it; the rough edge of my gnawed fingernail might wake her.

Over the next days, fighter jets screamed overhead. Their fierce rumbles protected the city against another attack—day and night— each one bringing to mind a tumble of fireballs from a red sky, recalling the apocalyptic visions I had as a child, brought on by severe midwestern thunderstorms. During the day, the jets would startle me into a nervous duck and cover that Jane could bring me out of with a firmer grasp of my hand. I nearly collapsed once on Broadway, but she held me up.

At night while I slept the roar could take on real form, and my dreams became all blazes and smoke. Fat cartoon bombs crashed down, killing scores of non-cartoon people. Photos from the *New York Post* came to life as office workers rained down in pairs, holding hands. And, of course, planes slammed into buildings.

For the next several nights we took turns. First my heart would race; I would shake in the dark. Later Jane would. If my dreams didn't wake me outright, her sudden trembling often did. My breathing would become shallow and quick. Although just as in the day, she could usually—without a word—reach out and take my hand a little tighter. I would fall back to sleep. Holding the back of Jane's head had the same effect on her.

In his first letter to the Corinthians, St. Paul famously says that as children we speak and understand as children, implying, of course, that there is a better, fuller way for adults to be. In other words, there is a time to put away childish things.

Yes, it's true that in the Gospels Jesus welcomes children to him, as children, and claims for them the kingdom of God, even identifying the simplicity and the purity of a child to be a kind of key. Speaking with Peter's son, Sam, on the phone once a week—always a story about what he ate with his dad or the games he played with his friends in the park down the block—is a good reminder that kids can, in their own way, know the sacredness of life: in this case, food, parents, and friends. Yet since in the same stories Jesus is never consistent in describing where the kingdom is or when it will come, and as a Christian I've chosen to take most seriously his many pronouncements that *God's kingdom is here*, to me these claims on the world, here and now, made for the sake of children, sound very familiar. They come not just from Jesus, but also from the mouths of economists, educators, and environmentalists alike, from the president of every senior class to every president of the United States: The world belongs to our children. And while we appreciate that children come into this world in all their simplicity—finding it everything from comic to beautiful—we discourage adolescent thumb sucking, teenage baby talk, and twenty-something make-believe friends. As September 11 demonstrates—for me, perhaps more clearly than any other moment—the world we've claimed for our children is far more complicated than most of us even know. And if we know this world as God's kingdom, or better, God's creation, childish approaches to faith and simple, say, unilateral, solutions to world problems just will not suffice. Yet even so, it's rare that religious people, as such, ever actually encourage each other to grow up. Growing up, I never was.

This is perhaps easiest to see among those who take the Bible at its literal word, or in communities—like the one in which I was raised—where being religious involves mostly recitation in church, where a dull yet adamant minister attempts to get his congregation to sit still while he instills the fear of what God the Father might do to us when he gets home—or, as I might have put it back then, when we go home to the Father. And as much as it means that we should put away the childish reading habits that have turned Genesis into a science textbook and the Gospels into an honest-to-God history lesson, growing up religiously depends on something more, on establishing homes of our own, say, and having faithful adult relationships, beyond the reach of what is commonly known as sacred, with friends as much as with lovers. This is the religion we should be teaching our children—not that God made the world in seven days, or that Jesus actually resurrected from the dead. Not that God has placed restrictions on whom we can love, and how (or when) we can love them. Not even that God, somewhere, acts like an actual father, fortress, or shepherd; and certainly not that he presides as Lord over an actual kingdom, with palaces for all the good people to go when they die.

These kinds of myths, the richest source for religious teaching that we have, are important only for what they reveal about our obligations to one another, about how to be friends, parents, and, also, how to be lovers. "We need myths," writes Karen Armstrong, a former Catholic nun turned religion scholar, "that help us to create a spiritual attitude, to see beyond our immediate requirements, and enable us to experience a transcendent value that challenges our solipsistic selfishness." As religious adults in the world, we experience spiritual *attitudes*, not spirits; we seek transcendent *value*, not transcendence. And selfishness, not sex, and not Satan—although we may call it that—is the enemy.

Our attitudes and values help us overcome that solipsism (which we often see in children), move beyond ourselves, and ultimately shape our search for meaning in life while facing reminders all the time—often dramatic events we cannot ignore—that death is coming. At our best, through this movement out of ourselves, the very act of imagination that myth inspires, we may strive toward limitless compassion and soulfulness while facing up to the reality that we may not actually possess an eternal soul at all. In the end, through the metaphors of spirit and Satan, transcendence and the soul—not to mention, yes, the will of God and even God himself—religion, and the myth that supports it, gives us helpful shorthand to talk about our potential to love and serve one another.

Our mythmakers have always been nothing if not imaginative, and as Armstrong contends, their most creative work is, like our best novels, "infused with the spirit of compassion . . . [and] respect for the sacredness of all life." And with regard to these myths, if we're going to be truly religious adults, we ought to reject the ascetic, world-hating impulse of celibacy, for example, the egotism at the root of our longing for eternal life, and the selfishness we find in childish literalism. We can reinterpret our old myths, or where that becomes impossible—as I see it, for example, with Jesus' uncharacteristic and sinful rejection of Mary Magdalene in the Gospel of John—jettison old, lifeless stories and create anew.

Peter recently sent me D. H. Lawrence's bizarre little two-part novel *The Man Who Died*, in which Christ, the man who died, may never have died at all. Crucified and then laid to rest in the same "carved hole in the rock" from John's Gospel, Jesus wakes "numb, and cold, and rigid, and full of hurt, and tied up." He'd been hurting for days, through his long sleep. And just as Jesus from the Gospels did, Lawrence's Jesus rises and returns from the dead. But in *The Man Who Died*, he rediscovers a resoluteness in the world that he had rejected according to Christian mythology, embodied in a crowing cock freeing himself at dawn, precisely the moment Jesus had been raised the previous day.

> As he came out, the young cock crowed. It was a
> diminished, pinched cry, but there was that in the voice
> of the bird stronger than chagrin. It was the necessity to
> live, and even to cry out the triumph of life.

In Part One of *The Man Who Died,* through encounters with Madeleine (Magdalene) and a peasant, Jesus reconsiders his life and mission, recasting the whole of it as a sort of insidious confusion marked by "the dread insomnia of compulsion" that marks every contact in society. The peasant offers him money in the same words Jesus uses in the parable of the prodigal son—"All that I have is yours"—yet the exchange saddens Jesus as he sees that the man's "eyes were cunning and sparkling with hope of greater rewards in money, later on. True, the peasant had taken him in free, and had risked getting no reward. But the hope was cunning in him." So, it is not the world, or the "seethe of phenomena," that Lawrence's Jesus rejects when he echoes John's Gospel, saying, *Noli me tangere!* First, he is still in too much pain to stand any physical contact. But more, he sees in his former days the selfishness and greed of the "little, narrow, personal life." He says to himself: "I tried to compel them to live, so they compelled me to die. It is always so with compulsion. The recoil kills the advance. Now is my time to be alone." And only by being alone and by killing the ego could this Jesus escape the compulsions that were the greatest sins of the world—his own sin, he realizes, and the sins of his society. Only in the appearance of death—and his own experience of it, and his coming out on the other side—could Jesus escape the "ultimate fear of death" that had made men like the peasant mad, ever crazed by cunning hope: "It was the mania of cities and societies and hosts, to lay a compulsion upon a man, upon all men. For men and women alike were mad with the egoistic fear of their own nothingness."

Before Jane, I was as mad as the peasant, as sinful as the Jesus of John's Gospel. I lived to preserve the stainless ego that I called my soul, which is not really living at all.

Of course, I still feared dying. September 11 was as close as the apocalypse had ever come, visiting me every night. And, if my calendar represents an accurate record of how I keep time, the world seemed to stop that day. After TUES 11 SEPT, the rest of the pages are blank. For months. No dinners, no parties, no performances planned; and no one appears at all.

This was a different world. There were no more to-do lists. There was nothing left to do.

Except, of course, to have sex for the first time, which Jane and I did the night after our next radio show. We'd played music again. We'd made out during Television's "Marquee Moon." And we both wanted more after our long bus ride home. I was nervous. I'd just turned twenty-five. It was terrible and embarrassing. There is little more to say than, as with everyone, it could only get better . . . *I prayed.*

In Part Two of Lawrence's novel, apparently freed of his fear of his nothingness, Jesus is reborn and sets out on his way "from the invisible snows of Lebanon" where he discovers the temple of Isis. Yet in his encounters with the priestess of Isis (*"I am risen!"* he says, and, yes, they have sex), he realizes that the temptation to live outside of cities and societies and hosts is as egoistic and narcissistic as a life of compulsion: "For the death aloofness is still upon me, and I cannot escape it," he says.

Contact itself, Jesus realizes, is not coercive; contact without true compassion is. As the priestess touches him, soothing the scars of his crucifixion with oil, she becomes absorbed in her task. Jesus finds within her the "pure search," a longing or yearning that is finally capable of love because it seeks nothing more than to imagine the situation of another. Jesus is able to overcome his own solipsism when he realizes through this contact that "she has another consciousness"; she both has a consciousness separate from his and also, in that moment, "she is making herself completely penetrable," imaginative and attentive enough to contain his consciousness in addition to her own. "Life," he concludes, "has brought me to this woman with warm hands. And her touch is more to me now than all my words. For I want to live—"

When a fear of death consumes you as it consumed me immediately after the attacks (along with the fear that I might die a virgin), you want to live and you seek to sustain life, run toward it, figure out how messy it really is, and discover what you've been missing all these years in never really giving yourself to another person, never really growing up. While my childhood fears had always been assuaged by what would be the glorious return of Jesus and the promise of my *own* eternal life—that in dying I would not die—I suddenly, and finally, had a reason to live that mattered more. I wanted to live—not forever, but for her.

EPILOGUE
— PB —

As long as I've known him, Scott has had trouble with women. And without question it's almost completely his fault. One late-spring afternoon, several years after his relationship with Jane finally ended, I got what had become a familiar phone call. This one, though, had an air of resignation to it. Scott was on the line to tell me that he and a woman he had been seeing had broken up. I was actually surprised by this one. I'd had big hopes for her. Lisa had all the right attributes: a professional artist (theater director), twenty-five (we had agreed long before that this was the cutoff), independent, beautiful, and, surprise, Christian. They had been friends for a long time, and at some point it just made sense that they start dating. But things quickly went awry. Typical things, typical for Scott, at least. She was just coming out of another relationship. She had known Scott as a friend for too long. Could she transform him into a lover? But most important, with all the people in his life he loves, would she ever feel special?

When we first met, there were some immediate clues pointing to turmoil in this part of his life. Most of his friends were women. He would often see two or three different people on any given night, each at a different time. I would get exhausted just listening to him tell me about an average Saturday night: drinks with a few friends, then a movie. Afterward a party. Then back at his house with a few more friends, talking until the sun came up. And there was always a close woman friend he had spent much of the evening with. While he never considered these "dates," it wasn't always so clear for the women he was with. He might not have known it then, but from what I could gather, it seemed to me all his women friends were secretly in love with him. Because Scott loves them all equally, he often finds himself unable to make a truly special place for the woman he does become romantically involved with. He doesn't want anyone to feel left out. But real monogamy means having to let go of all kinds of love affairs.

Losing his virginity was, in a sense, to give up a love affair with a particular idea of God. Remaining a virgin heightened Scott's vision of himself and his relation to the world. Like fasting and other spiritual disciplines, celibacy can produce a kind of altered state of being. But in matters of love (and sex) I sometimes worry that Scott is also seeking a kind of altered state, that he believes there is some transcendent experience. I fear he may be searching forever. For Scott, love cannot exist without God; his pursuit in love is perfectibility. But love requires sacrifice, one that I am not always certain he's willing to make. At one point, Lisa had Scott draw up a chart of all his friends. I imagine it looked like some great genealogical tree, Scott the patriarch and all his friends flowing downward, interconnected like a huge family. Where in all of this would a lover see herself? Lisa would have wanted to be placed at his side as the primary companion, part of the house all the others call home. But she probably saw herself as just one of many branches, twisting away from the center.

A month or so later, Scott was dating someone new. I was pleased to discover he hadn't known her before. She wasn't already a friend. And then, like clockwork, he took her to a party where a dear friend he had dated for a short time was going to be. The next day Scott received an angry e-mail: How could he be so insensitive as to bring a date? Scott, of course, saw no need to defend himself, but also hoped this didn't spell the end of an important friendship. No one, it seemed, saw the actual underlying message: Scott, why couldn't you have just been a priest after all?

I lost my virginity at fifteen, around the same time I lost most of my other innocence. My first lover and I tried to remain friends over the years, but foreshadowing much of my sex life to follow, eventually she decided she didn't want even that. Losing my virginity early didn't make me any more adept at relationships than Scott. I just have a longer track record of failed and sometimes reckless endeavors. And I didn't end up with a string of ex-girlfriends as friends.

Through many debacles and much prayer, it became apparent that monogamy is about more than sleeping with one person at a time. Monogamy, like celibacy, is a commitment to a spiritual value. And like any real spiritual value, it's one that involves great risk. So much of who you think you are is altered. I went into my marriage with my wife, Amy, believing myself to be patient, slow to anger, kind. Living with Amy day after day, having to negotiate everything from how not to wash whites and colors together to intense fights over using the "wrong tone," I discovered I am severely impatient, sometimes prone to angry outbursts, often uncaring, even capable of being mean. Gradually, this profound encounter with Amy had to begin to reflect a relationship with God, and so I slowly worked myself to the other side, a place where I have to try to quickly recognize when I am being annoyed, temperamental, unkind. Once I thought I was a sensual and skilled lover, only to find that sometimes I am selfish and passive. Learning to respond not to some idea of a woman's body, but to Amy's in particular, I have to do the work to become more adept where it actually matters.

I have often tried to tell Scott that this monogamy thing is a hell of a lot of work, but I'm not sure he really listens. He's traded celibacy for what might be an even more difficult path.

THE MARRIAGE PROPOSAL

— *PB* —

MARCH 31, 1998, was a partly cloudy evening. Amy and I were having dinner in a local pub. She was eating her burger, and I was secretly praying. It was a type of prayer I rarely ever say, a prayer asking God to alter reality. I was praying, begging really, that God clear the sky of clouds. I knew intuitively this kind of prayer was futile. God does not act in the world as I was praying for him to do on that night. God does not really part waters, cause earthquakes, save some people from burning buildings and let others die. But I was asking him then to clear the sky entirely so I could ask Amy to marry me while she gazed at the moon through a giant telescope. I was also praying for something else. God had to give me a stamp of approval on what I was about to do. I was about to choose monogamy. I had struggled with this as long as I have struggled with God. I needed a little support from on high.

Amy and I had just signed a lease on an apartment. A few months earlier we had decided to live together, and immediately after that I decided I would ask her to marry me. It seemed the only sane thing to do. I was getting too old for "girlfriends" and the eventual moving in together. I had even been engaged once before to someone else, but that was just a game we were playing, something new to call what we were doing. I was also finding myself tired of being in pain over women, tired of causing pain through my infidelities, and tired of my relationships with other people creating a huge gulf between me and God. This is where God is most often found—in relation with other people. If I couldn't get this right—if I couldn't be faithful in a relationship—I would never get it right with God.

Of course, one of the core Hebrew myths, the story of Adam and Eve, is about a relationship. Surprising though it may be, the creation of man is told twice in Genesis. In the first instance, the author of the creation story makes sure to note that the primal man, a kind of perfection of God's image, is not something that exists alone with God: "God created man in his image, in the image of God he created him, male and female He created them." In the following chapter the story is told again, but this time Adam is created first and Eve is formed later, only after God notices Adam's loneliness. Some scholars suggest that this second telling is merely a gloss on the first, but that seems like a bit of a quick rationalization for what is really a huge inconsistency. This second story is problematic on a number of other levels, not the least of which is the sentiment that women are dependent on men for their very existence. But as myth, the story still resonates in important ways. The primal relationship—partnership in the world with other people—is one in which we are mutually dependent on each other. Even though Eve arises out of Adam's body, he in turn must "cleave" to her and they become "one flesh." Nevertheless, the first mention of "Man" is one in which human beings, as first imagined by God, are *in relation*. That "male and female" reflect God's image suggests further that God is something that only exists in some kind of relationship. There might be times when we come to God alone, but to be human—to be part of God's creation, which means to be part of the world—we must be in relation with others.

When these relations go awry, however, especially in situations famously described by the Jewish philosopher Martin Buber as an I-It relationship, which he opposes to an I-Thou one, we encounter problems. The former relationship, as Buber puts it, is when we treat other people like objects. When we objectify another person, it's not possible for our relationship to become a vehicle for becoming more engaged in the greater world. What I once thought was love, a relationship that should have deepened my experience in the world, was more often than not obsessive and compulsive. My focus on the other person was simply a reflection of myself, of my desires, my fears, my anxieties. Being truly in relationships with others occurs when, according to Buber, "No set purpose, no greed, and no anticipation intervene between I and Thou." And the greatest reflection of this extends to our relationship with God: "Meeting with God does not come to man in order that he may concern himself with God, but in order that he may realize meaning in the world."

Amy and I had met two years earlier. What began as a love affair quickly started looking like a relationship, which for me often meant the end of romance, the end of the quickening of the pulse, the end of eager and curious sex. And so to be true to myself, I fled. But something about Amy kept drawing me back, and so we agreed to remain friends. Of course that rarely works out, and soon we were sleeping together again, and soon I was panicking all over again until finally Amy said good-bye to all that. I did not see her for six months. I continued on as I had before with a few other women, starting things up and then bailing when it looked like those initial feelings of intense desire were starting to wane. And all that time I thought about Amy. One night, near my birthday, she paid me a visit and we agreed to try again. I was so tired, so lonely, and so in love with her that I realized if I didn't make this thing work, I would never really be happy.

Coming to this decision was very practical. I simply couldn't imagine myself without her, as much as part of me tried to deny it. I have at times felt the same about God. I know God is a deep and abiding reality in my life, and yet sometimes I do everything I can to avoid him. God has been more patient than Amy was, and rightly so. Eventually she said that if I wanted to be with her at all, I had to be with her in full. And that's when I realized Amy was the one worth changing for. With Amy, if I wanted to be happy, I had to first be a *mensch*.

The right little antique jewelry shop was all I needed. I found an art deco setting with a fleck of a diamond, and I paid the lady behind the counter with a mix of certainty and dread. As I walked home with the ring in my pocket, it started to rain. I ran to a pay phone and called my dad and asked him what I was supposed to do now. He said, "Ask her to marry you. But first get out of the rain."

Once I had the ring I knew I had to do something big, something to let her know I really meant it. Every day I passed the Harvard Science Center and would look up at the two domes that housed the telescopes. So I started making phone calls. When I explained what I wanted to do, the person on the other end of the line was always confused at first, unable to help me, and would gently tell me to call someone else. Eventually I made my way to a graduate student who hung around the telescopes at night in case one of the faculty or visiting scientists wanted to come up and use them. He agreed that for about fifteen minutes he would let Amy and me into the Science Center to look through a telescope that he would have trained on the moon. He was only a little grumpy, but he said he would be there anyway, and as long as I didn't advertise the fact that he was letting me up there, it would be okay. I gave him a date, March 31, and said I would see him then. Now all I had to do was figure out a way to get Amy over there and hope it wouldn't be a cloudy night.

Sitting at dinner, I did my best not to appear visibly anxious. I kept looking out the window and glancing at my watch. Thirty minutes before we were supposed to arrive at the Science Center, the moon was becoming less and less visible. I excused myself from the table and from a pay phone called the graduate student. He asked if I could postpone, pick another time. "You might not see anything," he said. I started to panic and to doubt the whole project. Maybe this was God's way of telling me I was not ready, that my heart was a clouded thing made foggy by my libido and my fear. I said, "No. It has to be tonight. We're on our way."

Back at the table, I began to pray. Amy was talking and I was on conversation autopilot, dropping in a few well-timed "uh-huhs" and "mm-hmms." But to God I said, "I never ask for anything specific, I try never to pray for myself, but please give me this. Please, God, give me this."

I paid the bill and Amy and I walked out of the restaurant into the cooling night. She asked where we were going. I said she would know when we got there. I was hoping I would, also. I have had a lot of trouble with love in the past. I was hoping that God would show me the way out of that, into a new life of monogamy and, hopefully, contentment.

While Scott is the pure product of an all-American, rural Wisconsin, Catholic upbringing, where a virgin can give birth and other miracles abound, I am the pure product of a Northeastern, urban-fleeing, suburban Jewish background, where the only miracle was that you could get bagels and real lox outside of Brookline and that everyone's parents had either a copy of *The Joy of Sex* or *Our Bodies, Ourselves* hidden under the bed.

I was born in 1967, the youngest of four children. My oldest sister, Lisa, is ten years my senior. My brother, Eric, was born seven years before me, and my sister Karen three. Growing up, I watched them pop around the house like firecrackers, always looking for a way out of the suburbs, a way into experience. This was the birthright of the sixties and seventies. Experience. Freedom was only the means to get experience; it was not really the end everyone said it was. Freedom not for the sake of being free, but to live as you wanted so that you could experience the world. I was too young to understand what it was my brother and sisters wanted so badly, but at every moment they were reaching for more, taking more risks. They stayed out later and later, seeing how far they could take it. On the night of his bar mitzvah, my brother actually smoked a cigarette in our bedroom, letting the smoke waft out through an open window. But you could still smell it everywhere. I think he secretly wanted to get caught, just to be able to have the argument with my parents: "But why can't I smoke? You smoke! I can do whatever I want! I'm not a child anymore! Fine then, I'll leave!" Because leaving is what all the youth of the sixties and seventies really wanted anyway. And, of course, there was sex. And it was always sex with people my parents disliked or distrusted. So my siblings snuck out of the house and sometimes called later from whereabouts unknown, repentant, crying.

This sixties legacy of sexual promiscuity didn't do love relationships much good. My generation still often wants love to burn us up and keep burning, an eternal fire between ourselves and our lovers. We want love to be transcendent, and when it starts to show signs of immanence, of dailiness, we feel cheated. We easily live love as another form of excess. For a while, after I got clean and sober, I thought love and sex, the only other things that made me feel as crazy and wasted as drugs, might be what would carry me to heaven. This meant that I would go from relationship to relationship, fleeing one when the light dimmed in any way, getting into something else just as quickly when I felt like the flame had been extinguished all over again. The little ring burning a hole in my pocket in the restaurant was the antithesis to all this. A humble little diamond with almost no weight at all. You had to look carefully even to see it. But it was brighter and hotter than any torch I'd ever carried before.

I held Amy's hand and led her down the street. She was puzzled but curious. About five blocks from the observatory, I asked her to close her eyes and slowly led her down the sidewalk. All the while I looked at the sky and watched as the clouds gave no hint of clearing away anytime soon. I could see the moon peeking out, its edges becoming radiant as it was slowly covered again. She stumbled here and there, and I was trying to quicken our pace, trying, it seemed, to outrun something. I must have convinced myself somehow that if I didn't ask her tonight, I would never ask. If I was supposed to ask her, the sky would clear, and if it stayed cloudy, I should bring the ring back to the shop. I once relied so much on this kind of superstitious thinking, but now it was failing me. This couldn't really be the way the universe worked, could it? I could feel the doubt swimming in my stomach, slowly making its way to my heart. So I swallowed hard and kept walking.

When we arrived at the building, I looked at Amy with her eyes closed. I began to understand that I didn't need the sky to clear at all, because this was not what my prayer was really about. I was certainly going to ask Amy to marry me, with or without a telescope, but when I prayed I was asking to have a relationship with

God as well. I didn't really believe that God would or could make the sky clear or bring on a thunderstorm if he wanted to stop me. I didn't believe that God would change the weather just for me, but I believed in God enough to ask. I encountered God not in a transcendent moment but in an actual worldly moment, in my desire for help with my actual life. The one time I prayed for direct intervention, it was for something that I didn't even believe in; what I wanted from God was simply a real connection to him, not the miracle I was asking for. It was as if I was reaching out toward a friend to say, "I am about to ask this woman to marry me. Make sure you got my back, okay?"

As for Amy, I wanted so much for this to be a moment of spectacle, of dramatic certainty. I would give up all the rest, like I had given up the drugs and the alcohol and all the other excess. I would give up the fighting against discipline and ritual and getting up at a decent time every morning. But I would not give up romance. I would not give up the idea that I could lasso the moon and bring it down to my lover. So I prayed one more time, to myself, and brought her inside, into the elevator, to the top of the building where the student I had spoken with was waiting. He opened the door and showed us in to a massive room with a ladder reaching up to the giant telescope, a huge, long tube reaching out toward the sky through a hole in the domed ceiling. I let Amy open her eyes, and without a word she climbed the ladder and pressed her eye up to the eyepiece. I put my hand in my pocket, wrapped my fingers around the ring, and breathed.

As Amy stood on the ladder, I walked up a few rungs behind her. I opened up the box and held the ring up, shining a little flashlight I had brought along on the tiny diamond, hoping the light would make it look slightly bigger. I asked Amy what she saw. "It's the moon," she said quietly. The rock she was gazing on was far bigger than the one I had in my hand, but I decided to go for it anyway. "Amy," I called up to her. "Will you marry me?"

As with my marriage, or at least the leap of faith into marriage, where God is concerned I constantly have to make a leap of faith back to him despite all the distractions, both spiritual and worldly. The spiritual distractions are almost harder to relinquish because I have entertained so many strange and occult ideas throughout my life, some of which have been harder to shake than others. In marriage, as in faith, the lesson to be learned is not to make the phone call, not to get out all the old letters, not to Google the names of ex-girlfriends.

Every day I renew my commitment to my marriage when I wake up and see Amy in the bed next to me. But even with a daily prayer life, renewing the commitment to God is more difficult. I build up the detritus of material things, both in our home and in my mind. And so once a year, like an anniversary of sorts, I make a new vow to God during Yom Kippur.

Yom Kippur, known as the Day of Atonement, is a spiritual island. It happens once a year, and on this day Jews are required to inhabit a difficult religious space. On Yom Kippur we are commanded to fast, not wear garments made with leather, not to bathe or wash for pleasure, to refrain from work and sex. But most important of all is that Yom Kippur is a day of intense prayer, a day to recount our sins, to ask for forgiveness, and again establish a commitment to God and the commandments.

The first time I fasted on Yom Kippur and went to synagogue was in my late twenties. Growing up I only knew that this day was an important one, but there was not much else my family did about it except have a dinner on the night it ended. I had been behaving badly in relationships and feeling disconnected to any kind of spiritual practice. I had been making promises to God about this and that, and always felt like I was falling short. As I sat in the temple, surrounded by people I didn't know, I opened up the mahzor—the High Holiday prayer book—and it felt like a cold weight in my hand. I defiantly waited for something to happen, knowing nothing would. I wouldn't settle for anything less than a miracle. I was thinking, here I am, God. Let's see what you got. And then he gave it to me.

The Yom Kippur service begins with a prayer called the *Kol Nidre*, which means "all vows." The prayer reads, "All vows, oaths, and promises which we made to God from last Yom Kippur to this Yom Kippur and were not able to fulfill—may all such vows between ourselves and God be annulled. May they be void and of no effect. May we be absolved and released from them. May these vows not be considered vows, these oaths not be considered oaths, and these promises not be considered promises." I heard this. I said this. And I wept.

For the first time in years I felt clean, not like I had been washed of my sins but rather that I had been freed of all the feelings of self-doubt and shame at not being whom I thought I was supposed to be. Then I felt ready to get down to the business of asking for forgiveness, of renewing my vows to God. As the evening went on, I listened to the chanting of the cantor and the congregation. I looked around at the sea of people, their white prayer shawls covering their heads, those same heads bobbing back and forth like little buoys on this ocean of prayer. And then I understood something else, witnessed another miracle. On Yom Kippur, Jews ask to be redeemed, but while there are moments in the liturgy devoted to personal reflection, most of the service is about the collective people. It's not as if I will be redeemed while the heavyset fellow with the stained white shirt sitting next to me might not be. We are all redeemed or none of us are. We may think we come to God alone, but to be fully redeemed we come to God together.

This is also how my love relationship, my marriage, reflects a state of holiness. In coming together, we are blessed by God in a particular way. Our home becomes a microcosm of community, and so in our home we must act as we would in the world, and in the world we must treat people as we would our family. It's no easy task. And so every year we ask to start over. We say out loud that we fell short of promises and commitments made, but we are ready to try again. And in my home I wake up each morning and understand the same thing when I look at my wife.

I have found out that neither God nor love is really possible for me without the other. Without my marriage I would otherwise be lazy in my obligations to God, looking for sex more than encounters with the holy, masturbating more than praying, eating out every night, undisciplined, lazy, and selfish. And without faithfulness to God, I would not be much of a mensch in my marriage. I would be more unforgiving, more defensive, quicker to anger, and would find it harder to forgive. Selfish in matters of sex, more distracted by my other desires, less likely to offer back rubs and hugs. All these things, the selfish and the selfless bits, are human to be sure, part of the natural ebb and flow of marriage, but I am someone for whom structure is necessary to keep myself from losing control. In other words, I need sobriety to be sober, monogamy to keep me faithful to my wife, and my belief in a personal God to keep me faithful to him.

Wynton Marsalis once commented on bebop, explaining that what appears to be something almost totally without form is actually very disciplined in terms of the structure the musicians must agree to play within. But within this structure, Marsalis went on, the musicians have unlimited freedom. Similarly, in all the places in my life where I thought structure was inhibiting and limiting, I've found true freedom. What I mistook in the past as freedom was almost always selfishness, obsession, and sometimes even addiction. In faithfulness to God, having given up excess as a path toward him, I have found a greater depth of belief, one that demands that I keep my obligations to the world and to my relationships. There is nothing limiting about this at all. In fact, to be a friend, a lover, a parent, and even a son requires an even deeper encounter with the holy than I found watching trails come off my hands. And in matters of love and sex, this was most true of all.

In my marriage to Amy there exists everything God wants me to be. First, I need to wake up at a decent time to get everyone ready for the day. I am often the first one out of bed, while once I had always slept until just minutes before I had to leave the house. The swirl of anxiety in my belly at facing the day, what Kafka called the most precarious moment for the human psyche, is something I feel every morning. But I get out of bed. This takes faith. Second, I need to take care of other people. Drugs and promiscuity were about taking care of myself, no matter how much I thought these things were leading me to a greater spiritual understanding or some kind of mystical experience.

Rabbi Joseph B. Soloveitchik, the twentieth-century Orthodox Jewish philosopher, wrote about his skepticism over transcendence as an authentic religious goal. The problem for Soloveitchik was that we are so easily seduced by the subjective nature of how we might achieve transcendence that we end up finding only abstractions and never develop a relationship with the world; we fall into a spiritual solipsism that cannot bring us into a relationship with other people. The only way to do God's will, he insisted, is to act in the world: "It is not anything transcendent that creates holiness but rather the visible reality—the regular cycle of the natural order." These cycles—waking, eating, working, sleeping—were things I used to balk at, thinking they kept me from experiencing transcendence. I still sometimes ache for that mystical experience, but what is most important for me to remember is that I always mistook it for something else; for the perfect high, the perfect glance across the room, the perfect fuck. But this perfection was nothing but an I-It relationship. What I have now with my wife, with my son, and with Scott is something that looks more like an I-Thou. These kinds of relationships deepen my experience in the world. This experience often has to be about giving rather than taking, waiting my turn, doing the dishes, and not calling old girlfriends.

After the wedding ceremony, Amy and I went into a small back room for the ritual known as *yichud,* when the bride and groom spend some time in private before first greeting the guests as a married couple. Long ago this was when the couple would actually consummate the marriage, and it is said that afterward in some communities the groom would appear holding a bedsheet stained with blood, proving to everyone his bride had indeed been a virgin. Amy and I decided it was best to wait until we got to the hotel room, and instead of having sex on the hardwood floor we opened the window and looked out over the city, holding hands, giddy and dizzy from what we had just done.

That night it didn't matter that neither of us was a virgin. When we made love for the first time as a married couple, it was as if I was absolved of all my sexual and romantic misdeeds. And in this way I was transformed. Buber explains that if a person has chosen worldly pleasure—power, lust, even nationalism—over God, simply replacing God with the desired object does not make one religious. The relationship with these "idols," as Buber calls them, is an "It" relationship, one that obstructs God. We cannot encounter God in the same way. This would be an "unholy sacrifice piled up on the desecrated altar." But when a quest for "the ever repeated triumph" of sex and romance is utterly transformed, we can find God in that relationship: "When a man loves a woman so that her life is present in his own, the [Thou] of her eyes allows him to gaze into a ray of the eternal [Thou]." It wasn't enough for me simply to be monogamous if I was bringing to Amy the same selfish desires I had brought to past love affairs. That would be a desecration. To love Amy begins by loving God, and loving God happens when I love Amy, not as an idol but as another encounter with the holy. This was where I was to find the transcendent experience I sought for so long. I didn't need to climb a ladder to the heavens. Instead I brought the moon down and gave it to Amy as a promise and a vow.

I would be a liar if I said there wasn't a part of me that sometimes wants to flee, that still believes God is only found in some solitary exploration of my desire. I still want to experience altered consciousness as a way of encountering the divine. What I have to remind myself is that I can still have this, and that it happens in the context of a marriage, in having met my obligations to keep my home clean, my family fed. Then when they are all asleep, I can turn off the lights and sit in the dark, and I can pray that God be revealed to me as something beyond the material. But I have to fight the urge to make this the only way I can know God, and to remember that in a few hours I have to get up, get dressed, and get on the bus. The world is waiting.

EPILOGUE
— *SK* —

It's true. Though a relationship's early, passionate throes usually involve keeping baker's hours, young children are far more exhausting than young love. Predawn light caught in the small of your lover's back is all that remains of the night; the day finally ends here, you're spent, and you sleep, if only for a few hours (which is all the sleep you need). Predawn light reflected in the snotty face of a child, though, after he's cracked your bedroom door a few hours too early and reached out for your face, is the start of a whole new day. And you can hardly open your eyes.

And so for all my late nights and the running around I do in New York, I'm never more tired than when I'm with Peter in Cambridge. He walks fast, even pushing a stroller. (The sidewalks on his block, a mess of crumbling cobblestones under constant excavation by the roots of old trees, leave a lot to be desired, but he and Sam persevere, with me tripping in tow.) And though I'm not one to sleep late—I'm not actually much of a sleeper at all—mornings seem to come faster at his house; this despite the fact that, if at all possible, I'll nap in the afternoon. Plus the whole house is usually dark by eleven p.m., which gives me eight good hours of sleep before Sam appears at the side of the couch expecting me to make room so we can watch television together. I help him blow his nose.

And after that, yes, the world is waiting.

Now, it's the naïve, self-absorbed child who often has a difficult time conceding that his parents had a life, much less separate, romantic lives, before he was born. But never having experienced Peter's romantic fumblings before Amy (and, yes, ultimately before

Sam), part of me has a hard time imagining it too. This is the only life I've ever known Peter to have.

The first time I called, his machine picked up and he announced himself as a husband and new father: "Amy, Peter, and Sam aren't home right now." And while he's occasionally mentioned hard times with Amy, often arising from their not taking enough time alone together, concerns with careers and money, or less often Peter's ongoing struggle against superstition, their marriage (and so their lives as parents) has always reflected nothing less than an encounter with the holy.

Peter's struggles with monogamy have never been apparent to me. Even a conversation we once had about pornography centered more on the ethical problems of contributing to a corrupting industry than on whether either of our fantasies about other women threatened our ability to have faithful relationships. We could finally agree that porn, like other tantalizing distractions, can be an enormous waste of time, and when confronted with endless and *necessary* constraints on how we spend our days—divided among our work, our families, our friends—this may be its most sinful quality. But even this understanding seemed to me then like a point of disconnect: Through it all, Peter was still nothing but a committed family man whose concerns with porn revealed no chink in the armor of his marriage. He was actually more concerned about those poor, young girls.

Ever since those days after I lost my virginity, Peter and I have talked about relationships and sex. But like a stubborn and unimaginative child, I've always resisted his insight and advice about the women in my life. The single romance I've witnessed in Peter's life has alone been a sort of lesson for me: In a sense, I have always known the very sum of his existence to be Amy, Peter, and Sam, and he's often been loath to talk much about any other women.

And I understand monogamy to be God's will for me in my relationships. Peter's marriage itself shows that love and such faithfulness is possible. Sam is all the evidence I need that I could be a father someday. Yet as comforting as that is to know, it's also been the source of great frustration as I've failed time and time again with young love.

For as long as I've known him, Peter has asked difficult questions about my friendships and romances with women: Aren't you, at one level, just being selfish, flattering yourself in having all these friends around, friends who deep down may really *love* you? What if you meet someone you really want, and need, to *change* for? Could you? Will you? *What would God have for you?*

Knowing only his relationship with Amy, though, and stubborn as a snotty kid in refusing to give Peter the credit he's due for having his own struggles with young love, it's possible I've never properly answered him.

Could I? Would I? What would God have for me?

I just haven't been able to say.

It's too bad, but someday I expect Sam will put a similar answer just as maturely:

Whatever, Dad!

The first time my mom mentioned wanting to date again was two years after my stepfather died. I'd made it my habit to talk with her every day since then—part of a promise I'd made my stepdad—and on this night, I just happened to be on my way to meet a woman at her apartment for a first date. (First and last, I should say.) There was someone in particular, my mom said, a teacher who worked with my brother. He'd also taught me in high school. Just as stand-up as the men she'd loved before; no one could disapprove, and the time seemed right.

In turn I told her about my date. "She has a Red Cross tattoo on her arm. And short hair." She could have guessed that much. But that was about all I knew.

Over the years since then, my mom and I have talked about all of my relationships, the conversations becoming increasingly candid in fits and starts, usually following her lead. On one visit, though, she finally broke through. "I'd like to spend my life with someone again. Someone to travel with."

"Would you get married again?" I asked.

"No," she said. "I'd like to sleep with someone, though."

Dating had been one thing; sex was another topic altogether. We'd never said a word about sex. And then she turned it on me: "I mean, I figure you've messed around."

Messed around.

I smiled, embarrassed and relieved. Because suddenly my mom and I were both singles looking for young love again, each desiring sex again. We were looking for companionship. Perhaps we all always are. I'd never again have to lie to her about where I'd spent the night. She'd always understand. I'd never have reason again to say: *Whatever, Mom!*

Considering my mother's life, knowing that she had known young love to mature into marriage—twice, in fact—and continues to seek it, makes me rethink my ability to answer Peter's questions about love and faithfulness.

Could I change?

Certainly.

Would I change?

I only pray.

What would God have for me?

Something like the love I see between Peter and Amy. Or the love my mother misses more than anything and the love she'll continue to seek. It's part of the love that asked me to call her every day. And the love they've all always hoped I'll find. Rather than struggle with monogamy, God's having me mature into it. And as an example he's given me Peter, and even more, the love of my two fathers for my mother.

THE TATTOO

— *SK* —

IT WAS A COOL, overcast Wednesday in the spring. Just about a year since my stepfather died. I had left the office by midafternoon and was standing under the building's awning with the smokers, out of the drizzle, to confirm my appointment over the phone. I dropped the design off yesterday, I explained. It had taken me months to decide how the letters would connect and overlap. The guy on the phone coolly assured me he would find it before I arrived. I had another copy just in case. I had been carrying the design with me for weeks, taking the advice given me to wait, and then wait some more, before making it permanent. I'd even given blood the day before in preparation: The Red Cross had rules that would keep me from donating for a year after this, plus I thought that one session with one long needle might ready me for the thousands of buzzing pricks I was about to face in taking on the indelible mark of a tattoo.

My bike was chained to a street sign; it would be a short ride. But then again so was home. I could still forget the whole thing. Leave my body alone, just the way it was. The way God intended, some argue. It would be painful. A feeling like I'd never felt before. It would burn. And it would last forever.

I unlocked the bike. Riding clears my head. I would decide on the way uptown.

Daredevil Tattoo is on Ludlow Street, on New York's Lower East Side. The place came highly recommended as clean, safe, and professional, yet still had the Fall and the Buzzcocks on heavy rotation. To me, Daredevil would be "the two cluttered rooms over a chiropodist's office on a back street," from Flannery O'Connor's story "Parker's Back," the shop where the sad hero, after narrowly escaping a fiery farm accident, has his back covered with a Byzantine Christ for his "plain, plain" pious wife, who sees his tattoo-covered body as a "heap of vanity." "She can't say she don't like the looks of God," Parker reasons. "She can't hep herself." Now, I wasn't worried about a wife—although Parker's wife is right, tattoos are vain—nor was I having this done for anyone else but me, necessarily. Still, I thought, my mother would hate it, and she would let me know in no uncertain terms. Although as much as she would cringe to see me permanently scarred, she would still have to love the tattoo. She wouldn't be able to help herself.

Zane, the friend who recommended Daredevil and inspired the design in the first place, had gotten his tattoo there: DOMINUS ABSTULIT inked in bold letters in a ring around his right forearm, and under that, MCMLXXXII. Job 1:21, from the Latin Vulgate. *The Lord taketh away.* His was an angry mark in memory of a father who, in 1982, worn out on cocaine, had slammed his car into a Northern California redwood. A note he left behind expressed regret at ruining his own life and the lives of his family—but he assured them that he was saved in Jesus Christ.

While I had to find my own mark, Job's complaint resonated with me, too. And I had to agree, 1982 was a pretty terrible year.

In 1982 my parents, Frank and Virginia, were both teachers.

By late May my father had already ended his semester at Alverno College, a Catholic women's college in Milwaukee; my mother was on maternity leave, taking care of my little sister. They'd always had their summers off, which is the main reason that both my sister and brother are teachers, and why I've always been somehow affiliated with a college, university, or, when I first came to New York, the seminary. We learn as children what is right and what to expect, like families traveling together and having summers off. This last summer before I would start school full-time, we were getting an early start. They took my brother out early and planned a trip to visit family in Florida before heading to the World's Fair in Knoxville, Tennessee.

My sister was just a baby then, too young for the long drive from Wisconsin, so my mother had arranged air travel for the three of us while my father and my older brother drove. This was Memorial Day weekend. Mom took care of the little ones, Sara and me. Dad went on a road trip with his namesake, Frank. Though we'd all arrive in Florida the same day, we had different destinations for the first days of the vacation, visits planned with different relatives in different parts of the Sunshine State.

Returning one rainy afternoon from a scallop-fishing junket, towing a small boat, my father and my brother, together with my aunt and uncle, were hit head-on by a drunk driver on slick roads. A photograph from the *Gainesville Sun* shows the hood of the car crushed from above; the boat had fallen from the sky. Another photo shows the other driver sitting in a squad car with the door open, his feet swung around and resting on the ground. He looks confused but unhurt. A police officer bends low in front of him, shining a flashlight into his eyes. Another cop stands against the squad car, staring down the photographer. Everyone in my aunt's car was injured that afternoon, my brother with a fractured skull, my uncle with a broken knee and elbow and jaw. My father died instantly in the front passenger's seat. He was thirty-nine.

We did not stay long in Florida; he would be buried in Wisconsin. I have two clear memories of the wake. First, I did not cry. I was too busy fooling around with my little cousins most of the afternoon, slowing down only enough to peer into the open casket, where I found my dad's pasty face and his well-groomed beard. Second, the Knights of Columbus, a quasi-secret Catholic fraternal organization and familial mainstay, stood at either end of my father's casket, still as the bouquets of flowers, holding swords and wearing regal capes. Had my dad stood guard over a dead Knight before? What could they possibly be defending that they would need swords?

In the weeks and months after the funeral, though, I grew confused. *Where did he go?* All I knew was what had been explained to me: My dad was in heaven with God. And in almost no time at all, to my imagination, this man became faultless: "On Earth as it is in Heaven," said the Lord's Prayer. No one could be more worthy of heaven than he was. He'd been honored like a king, or a saint.

Yet despite the assurances that my dad was with God, I missed him. I was devastated, wracked, I realize now, by an early bout with disbelief. *Where did he GO! WHERE!* And in the summer of 1982, a small seed was planted. I began to expect that men in my life would die young. (It didn't help that two years after my father died, his father did. And knowing me to be both gullible and overly sensitive, my maternal grandfather, with his dark and often mean sense of humor, regularly reminded me that when all his toenails turned yellow, he'd be gone too.)

My mother quickly gave away most of his clothing and possessions, and packed away the things she couldn't part with in an antique steamer trunk that sat at the foot of her bed my entire childhood. Its contents would be mine someday. A Milwaukee Braves autographed baseball. His pipe collection. A gavel he'd once been given during a race for an area judgeship (he lost). Rings for his tiny fingers. His own Knights of Columbus sword and cape. A crucifix and rosary. As often as I could, I undid the leather straps and metal latch of that trunk and looked for my dad, imagining my inheritance in a whole lifetime—short as it was—of miscellany.

Before taking the position at Alverno College, where he was working when he died, my father was an elementary school teacher. His first job was at a Catholic school teaching alongside my mother's cousin Roy, his best friend, who introduced him to my mom during a spring-break vacation one year—in Florida. My parents' engagement the next fall has become a bit of family lore, a story of my dad out drinking Pabst Blue Ribbon beer with Roy one Friday evening after work, planning a party at his parents' house while they were away. The two got to talking about my mother, whom my father had wooed over the summer with bundles of love letters that my mom still has safely tucked away. Out of the blue, he asked Roy to drive him to the airport.

"I'm going to propose to your cousin, Roy. You'll have to have these people over tonight without me."

"But Frank, it's at *your* parents' house!"

"I'm going, Roy. I'm going. Let's go."

So Roy threw the party. Frank went to Florida. Virginia said yes.

The family my parents started in suburban Milwaukee was a religious one, their children, of course, all cradle Catholics like they had been. For us there was weekly Mass, the observance of Lent with fish fries and giving things up, prayer before meals, and the sacraments. While it may have been frightening at times, faith was not complicated. This much I knew: Of course I would learn my catechism. I would be an altar boy. And this all had something to do with a real place called heaven. God was there. If we behaved we would go to meet him when we died. Scared and chosen, I sang my choruses of *Yes, Mother* and went to bed when I was told. I played nice. I never spoke out of turn. No way would I run with scissors.

At church we learned that God's son, Jesus Christ, was born in a manger, one time fed lots of people with fishes and loaves, prayed the Lord's Prayer (and not just said it, but *invented* it), ate a last meal with his friends, then was killed so he could be buried and rise again. That was the Resurrection, and the Resurrection, it seemed, was the point of it all. Jesus died for us because we were sinners. When he rose again, he saved everyone from sin and death. He made it possible for us to go to heaven someday. Jesus was the Savior, somehow God and man all in one. He saved my dad.

With my belief in the story of the Resurrection came my preoccupation with Revelation and the end of the world; Jesus would come again someday, and all the dead people would rise up from the ground. I imagined all the cemeteries emptied, everywhere, and this terrified me. Driving by a cemetery anytime after dark, especially after my dad died, I would duck my head beneath the car window so I could not see out, asking my mom to tell me when we had passed it. Anytime the sky took on a sort of ominous reddish color during electrical storms, I would panic that the end of the world was at hand, and, clinging to life, would hide in the basement under a table or behind the couch, my fear of God—or death, basically—taking hold in an unnatural fear of tornadoes.

Just as my own religious focus was narrow—death, Dad, heaven, a red-sky apocalypse, and Resurrection—the world of religion was small in my suburban town. My neighbors were mostly

Catholics, families I would see at church. All of them would someday crawl out of their graves for sure. My best friend's family was Lutheran, still Christians, and they would certainly all be resurrected. There was the small Methodist church on Main Street, where in high school I played drums with the youth group before heading to Catholic Mass at St. Thomas; the two black kids in town had been adopted by Methodist families, and my tennis coach played bass with me in that church band. As for Judaism, while I had heard stories from my grandfather about the "dirty Jews," I didn't actually meet a Jew until I was eighteen. And of Muslims, Buddhists, Hindus, et cetera, et cetera, et cetera, I heard nothing, ever. For all I knew, the whole world might have been Christian in one way or another—and good, because Jesus alone saved.

In the wake of my father's funeral and for years after, I conceived of God as something like a telephone switchboard operator, connecting people on earth with their loved ones in heaven. Catholic priests, I would learn, played a similar role, connecting their congregants and confessors with Jesus. In my nightly prayers I would dial up heaven and ask God to connect me with my dad, please. And he would. Then God would leave us alone to talk. Those days, I believed less in God than in Saint Frank James Korb.

In the years to come, though, any hope I had in coming to a deeper, less narrow, and more adult faith in God would depend on trying to let go of the "Saint" part of my father's name. To this day, however, I still carry with me some relics: a small pipe he used to smoke, a pin he wore.

The process of forgetting the saintliness I had granted my dad started with accepting, over time, that he had been a normal man with normal faults, sins, and failings. Accepting such a thing is especially difficult when your whole life people tell you how much you remind them of him. At twenty-nine, I have his crow's-feet and his smile lines, his groomed beard. Admitting his failings and weaknesses—his temper, his political and social conservatism, which I had to believe without having seen—somehow demands admitting my own: the pride in feeling chosen not despite but because God had taken my father, or the "heap of vanities" I was riding uptown for, to commemorate him.

But learning to let go of what shaped my early and easy understanding of God and the church—which, let's be honest, was knowing that my dad was not, in fact, gone, but just somewhere else waiting for me, or that he would someday claw his way out of the dirt to find me—suggests there must be a better way. There was more to find at Daredevil than endless vanity. A tattoo is a scar, after all. It actually makes you less perfect.

Following a short courting period and an even shorter engagement, my mother remarried three years after my dad died. The whole thing left no cache of love letters. Paul Alois Boglitsch, the friend of my father's sister Kathy, was forty and had never married before. He had lived with his mother in the years since his own father died, in great pain, of pancreatic cancer.

After the wedding Paul moved in with us, and we immediately took to calling him Dad. Paul raised us as his own children and, at my mother's insistence, had a vasectomy to prevent more of us. In the first years of his marriage to my mother, I occasionally experienced a faint sadness around him, perhaps related to my own loneliness, the lingering effects of having a dead father replaced by someone with a different, practically unpronounceable, last name. Still, I like to think it was actually a nascent compassion that Paul stirred in me simply through his humility and his example—never insistent, never rude. I doubt I really understood that he would be missing something in never having children of his own, in never adopting us, in knowing his place outside the seemingly impenetrable quartet my mother had formed with her brood. She was the disciplinarian, the comforter, the parent. If ever forced to choose, she would choose us over him. And Paul—above all else an endlessly charitable, self-sacrificing, and faithful man, and in these ways arguably more of a "saint" than my father ever was—accepted his role as long as he lived, disciplining his children only when we hurt his wife.

Yet despite all this, when he died he hurt my mother more than her children ever could.

In October 2000, Paul was diagnosed with inoperable colangiocarcinoma, cancer of the bile duct related to a massive abdominal cyst he had had removed the first year of his marriage, which had left him with a great pink scar. He'd almost died back then.

I was called home from New York. I manned the phone, explaining to all the relatives—out of my mother's earshot—that Dad was very sick again. I spent those days with him at the hospital watching the 2000 National League Championship Series, which pit my New York Mets against the St. Louis Cardinals. My dad was rooting for the Cardinals, apparently forgetting the World Series in 1982, when the Cardinals beat our Milwaukee Brewers, making that summer *even worse*. He seemed slightly resentful of me, as he saw it, for giving up my midwestern roots for big-city flash. The Mets would win the NLCS, but lose the World Series to the Yankees. I spent most of that fall in Wisconsin, missing the hoopla surrounding the subway series while my dad settled into nearly two years of chemotherapy, fifty-seven treatments, one for every year of his life. Over that time, he and I would both come to terms with death, which, for a Catholic raised on it, would mean giving up a whole lot right from the start.

And I started big, as only God would have it. I had never had a closer friend than Matt. Yet Matt was the first I let go.

One night, weeks after I had returned from Wisconsin after my dad's diagnosis, I sat in the basement bedroom of the duplex I rented in Brooklyn, my feet propped on the low shelves of a bookcase. Matt had *finally* called from Chicago, where he and his wife had just taken up home. They were young newlyweds; I'd been among the six people at their wedding, his "best man," not that there had been any competition. Not even his siblings had been invited. His father-in-law presided over the ceremony.

I knew my roommate very little at the time, apartment shares being fairly common among recent suburban transplants. When I had returned from Wisconsin with the final word that my stepfather was dying of cancer, this roommate made some requisite yet earnest inquiries as to how I was holding up. Did I need anything? With a near stranger my closest confidant, Matt's call from Chicago had simply taken too long.

But his tardiness was only half the trouble. Matt was an honest-to-God, God-fearing, born-again Christian. He should have been better than this. In the months before his wedding that year, he had been baptized in a swimming pool. His mission at the time was evangelism. If only we could all be as happy as he was, having "found Jesus." And it's true, he had never been happier in his life.

He suddenly seemed to know his Bible as well as I did, yet we knew it so differently. That night he argued from the Gospels. Matt shouted: Jesus gave sight to the blind. Healed the lepers. Raised Lazarus. Of course he could cure your dad. So I shouted back: *But those things didn't* really *happen! I don't believe those things!*

What was I saying? Was it true? By that moment, facing the certain death of another father, had I really stopped believing in miracles: the loaves and fishes, walking on the water, Jesus' curse on the fig tree? When had *this* happened?

New Testament classes at the seminary had offered me a more rational approach to the Scriptures than I'd ever taken before, and introduced me to the historical Jesus, the living, walking, and talking radical Jewish teacher. The earliest Gospel—Mark, written in the late sixties A.D.—didn't tell of Jesus' miraculous birth or his Resurrection. The later Gospels all played up the mythic elements to reassure believers that Jesus was the messiah and would return. But he hadn't, and maybe now, I thought, he never would. I read over and over a book by my seminary's most celebrated former faculty member, Dietrich Bonhoeffer. His *Letters and Papers from Prison*—written from a Nazi prison at Tegel between April 1943 and October 1944—explained that "Man is summoned to share in God's sufferings at the hands of a godless world." God as I knew him had disappeared; Jesus had lost his magic, and, just as it was for St. Paul, his *power was made perfect in weakness*.

As an adult, I'd found an urban, more liberal and socially conscious church than the one where I'd grown up. Week to week, my priest was beginning to sound more and more like Bonhoeffer, reminding me during worship that the religious communities serve God by serving the poor and the outcast, the sick and the widowed. And so, even in church, Jesus was less God than ever before. Biblical miracles meant far less than the ones we were called to perform every day. My priest often ended his homilies: *Now go!*

That night, neither Matt nor I was able to explain why we found the other's belief so frightening and dangerous. All he could say was that if only I'd seen this woman at his church, bent over, her spine filled with tumors one day, and then, after the miracle of prayer, the next day her doctors could not find a thing. He insisted that if only I'd love him enough—and by *him* Matt meant God and my dad, both—cancer was fully treatable with prayer, or better, by a minister's laying-on of hands. Through prayer and loving God, he repeated.

What happened, I asked him, to love's being patient, kind, not rude, not insistent on its own way?

What happened to love fucking calling a few weeks earlier?

Our conversation went on for hours. I was fighting a little cross-country holy war from my basement in Brooklyn, and by the end, trading biblical advances and parries, I was wrecked. Matt had no sense of me as a Christian. Though how could he? I'd just denied the basis of his newfound faith. Miracles. He must have sensed that in denying the little miracles, I'd someday soon have to jettison the big one: Jesus' Resurrection. And in giving up that, I'd need no more life after death. Nothing eternal. Nothing permanent. Matt was right to fear I'd someday give up on any personal God to ground my faith.

My faith was already becoming more and more about the compassion of Jesus, the utter worldliness of his preaching, most notable in Luke's Sermon on the Plain, and Jesus' encounters with the poor and the lowly. You know, *blessed are the poor*, I said. My faith could not bear Matt's faith in the literalness of the Bible, the claims of belief in miracles. I could not bear the thought that my dad would be healed if only I loved enough. God could not work that way. And then I hung up, my entire faith turning on the hope that Luke's Jesus was right: *Blessed are you who weep.*

Pedaling to Daredevil, heading north on Water Street, the whole of downtown lived and raced behind me. I was in Chinatown at Canal Street, swarms of people on foot swinging their grocery bags filled with the produce that lines the streets, tourists walking against the lights. Behind me were the Manhattan and Brooklyn bridges, the financial district, the ferry ports; ahead was the rest of the city, going on for miles and miles. And I was alone, traveling and watching.

Praying. I found myself praying just by seeing the world as God's creation. Our inheritance. This is where God is.

I often feel I'm best on a bike, safe, in tune with the city. It's where I've learned to pay better attention to my everyday life and those around me. I've come to find the confusion and fragility, vulnerability and independence, of being *in* traffic more my speed, more fit for me as a believer, better reflecting the very nature of my belief. A bike seems to be a way to assert my belongingness here more completely, a way to be closer, more a part of the city's relentless living.

Admittedly, it is not perfect and not entirely safe, but that is so much the point. This sort of travel, a mix of reflection and prayer, vulnerability and mad aggression, the miracle of surviving the commute right in the middle of it all, is a pilgrimage of sorts. But this journey seems quite different from the old-fashioned version, in which the pilgrim hunts desperately—along a well-worn path— for some other place where God is because God cannot possibly be found here. I imagine the harrowing, mystical, and pious journeys of the religious of a long-lost time—probably through craggy Russian mountains—the hair shirts and bloody knees from all that crawling, uphill both ways.

My knees and elbows may be just as bloodied, sure—I've had my share of crashes—but I've gotten to the point that my desperate longing for God or faith or both can be based only on the hope that the search, as disciplined and faithful as those ancient journeys, must in fact be a worldly one we make up as we go, and one that at each moment finds God only in our commitments to the ethical life we've chosen by living here among so many others, all under so much pressure. This God is always where we are, waiting for us to serve him. We must nurse our fathers when they are dying. We must donate blood when a friend asks. We must believe, as my stepdad did, that we serve God in serving the poor. We must accept our inheritance of taking care of what is ours, loving God by loving our mothers, loving our neighbors, loving our enemies.

Mine is not a relativist belief but a responsive one, a pilgrimage in which the journey—complete with its off-key and off-color moments, and my ending up slightly broken or bloodied—is nothing but this whole life of prayer punctuated with fleeting miracles that could appear anywhere just so long as we are paying attention. Even after we face our tragedies—and we all do—there is nothing left for us to do but really belong here, take up or continue our own sort of vocational pilgrimages, and pray all the while. And by pray I mean live, more or less.

By the time I arrived at Daredevil, reminded of what the inky scar would mean, I'd decided to have the work done. In fact, I'd probably decided months earlier, when Paul died and, like Flannery O'Connor's Parker, I'd faced that great change in my life, "a leap forward into a worse unknown." There was nothing I could do about it.

I went back to Wisconsin when Paul finally needed a nurse. I packed a dark suit. And over the following weeks, my dad and I made a fairly regular routine of his home care. Together we showered and shaved him in the mornings. I was careful to protect his shrinking modesty with a towel. I applied new dressings to his abdomen. We sat in quiet. My dad and I talked. I prepared tiny, bland meals he could stomach. Or I held the bucket while he threw up. I found every baseball game on the television. I counted and delivered pills to him three times a day. I cleaned the port where they needled the chemotherapy. I positioned a pillow behind his aching back before driving him to the cancer center. It wasn't until his final two weeks that we ordered the gurney and he never left the family room.

The twenty months of almost weekly chemotherapy treatments had burned him bad, something I could hardly see while I was with him. Not until months after the fact, when I received in the mail some photos of him from this time, did I realize how flush he actually had gotten. Only then did I notice how deeply his eyes had sunk into his skull, how dark the shadows were, how square and bony his face had gotten, how he looked just like his mother when she died.

His look is the same in every picture. He tries to smile. He clenches his crooked, yellowing teeth. In two of the photos—taken by my mother at a cabin they'd built for their retirement together—he sits with me on the porch swing, gripping the wood for dear life. It seems impossible, but I'm laughing in both photographs. In one, I'm actually slapping my knee.

He is all bones under a brand-new white T-shirt hanging hollow off his collarbone, bunching up against the tubes sticking out of his abdomen and running over his belly and down into his pants. Bile would leak from where the tubes entered his body and through the dressings we taped to his skin every morning and every night. We had to buy new shirts often. Under his pants he wore bags to collect the bile that didn't leak down his belly. I drained the thick, bloody, shit-smelling fluid from the bags and flushed it down the toilet.

In the swing photos, his arms are skinnier than mine—and my

arms are *skinny*. In another photo, also taken on the front porch of the cabin, he sits alone on a plastic deck chair, looking sad, and his ears are huge. This man is dying. And he knows it. He can feel it. My very being there and no longer biding time in New York, my snapping photos, even my fat luggage containing my dark suit, reminds him.

One morning, eighteen months after his diagnosis—after I'd been home for six weeks—my dad's kidneys failed, leaving him lethargic and confused. We took him to the hospital, where, after hours of waiting, the doctor offered him the choice to stay in the hospital, supported by machines, and live for a month or more, or go home to die within the week. My dad chose to go home. He could hardly sit up. And that day we talked:

"You have to take care of your mother."

"We know. We will."

"You have to take care of your mother when I'm gone. She's already been through this once."

"Yes, we know. Don't worry."

That was the charge of faith, of humility and of selfless compassion. He spoke to all of his children as the faithful adults we were. Seemingly not concerned with his own salvation, nor fearful of death, not presuming a thing about God in the afterlife, Paul knew only his obligation to my mother, to his faith in the things of this world. He acted out that faith in awarding us our inheritance. This is what happens when we die. It was for me just as Philip Roth records in his memoir *Patrimony*, when he comes to terms with the death of his father, Herman, of brain cancer:

> Dying is work and he was a worker. Dying is horrible and
> my father was dying. I held his hand, which at least still felt

like his hand: I stroked his forehead; and I said to him all
sorts of things he could no longer register. Luckily, there
wasn't anything I told him that morning that he didn't
already know.

Paul said, Take care of all that I have loved after I'm gone. And
before he could no longer understand us, he knew we would.

Inheritance is not possession alone, but assuming responsibility.
And as with Roth, that began with taking care of him and what
he has, his suffering and imperfect body; the body that leaks and
betrays us, that grows cancer and loses control. This is, Roth concludes, "right and as it should be. You clean up your father's shit
because it has to be cleaned up, but in the aftermath of cleaning it
up, everything that's there to feel is felt as it never was before." All
that is mine is yours, my dad seemed to say, an echo of the father
from Jesus' parable of the prodigal son.

The parable, found only in the Gospel of Luke, is one of the best
known of the New Testament. It was one of my dad's favorites. A
man has two sons. The younger son requests his inheritance, the
share of his father's property that will belong to him. So the father
divides the property between the sons, and the younger famously
departs for a distant country and squanders his portion in "dis-
solute living." When a famine strikes the land, the prodigal son
finds himself in desperate need, and so takes the low work of
feeding pigs: "He would gladly have filled himself with the pods
that the pigs were eating; and no one gave him anything." Faced
with this squalor and destitution, he "comes to himself" and de-
cides to return to his father, beg forgiveness for sinning against
him and against heaven, and request that his father put him to
work. Upon the son's return, however, his father celebrates the

homecoming, kills the fatted calf, and then organizes a party of singing and dancing. Returning from the field and hearing the hubbub, the elder son complains against the father: "Listen! For all these years I have been working like a slave for you, and I have never disobeyed your command; yet you have never given me even a young goat so that I might celebrate with my friends. But when this son of yours came back, who has devoured your property with prostitutes, you killed the fatted calf for him!" The father corrects the elder son, reminding him of his real inheritance: "You are always with me, and all that is mine is yours."

This parable is widely taught for what it has to say about compassion and forgiveness and the promise of homecoming, for illustrating that it's never too late to repent, and for its final line, which I have so far left out: "We had to celebrate and rejoice, because this brother of yours was dead and has come to life; he was lost and has been found." And alternately, we are taught never to respond with the ugly jealousy of the elder brother—love is not resentful. Both sons are sinners, and in such different ways.

Yet what if the sons are actually more similar than different, both blind to the only real inheritance promised in the parable—a worldly one? Feeling the world as we've never felt it before. What if this parable has as much to say about our earthly inheritance, creation itself, as it does about radical compassion and the pitfalls of jealousy and resentment? What if we linger over the father's words, "all that is mine is yours," and understand this to be the better inheritance, the best lesson we could ever learn and our greatest desire? And what if we, like the sons, need only to be reminded—as I believe Jesus tries to do with this parable—that we have all already received our inheritances, by our births and not our baptisms (where we're told we "die with Christ"), and so in our lives and not our deaths? Christian faith would become radically different. Once we accept that our inheritance is the here and now, and that it's all that we've ever had, all that Jesus had—all that we'll ever have—then the things of this world can begin to be understood as holy, the real presence of God.

Focusing on confession and love of the here and now may be just the right way to stomach this Christian legacy I'm living under. I can let go of both the ancient miracle of the Resurrection and the modern miracle Catholics experience when priests change bread and wine into the real presence of Jesus in the Eucharist. In fact, I must let go of these most basic elements of Catholicism that point to the afterlife, salvation, and personal, eternal reward. But why? Religion scholar Karen Armstrong, who is also no longer interested in the afterlife, has answered this question well: The afterlife is about preserving your ego "eternally in optimum conditions." It's that sort of egotism that God would have us let go of, and that builds walls between people. Armstrong is right: "A lot of people see God as a sacred seal of approval on some of their worst fantasies about other people." And if faith obliges us to do the will of God, we can do nothing but lovingly strive, through humility and selfless compassion, to belong here, pay attention, and take care of each other.

If God is nothing—really *nothing*—but the demand that we live well here, compassion is the way, and compassion, by definition, demands humility and the end of egotism. This may mean finding the real presence of God not in any cup on any altar, where my tradition has forever said it is and where I've always looked, but rather in the mess of blood, ink, and petroleum jelly that would soon scar my right shoulder, compelling me never to forget my inheritance, or in the blood donated to a local hospital

and entered into the National Bone Marrow Registry while a friend
with leukemia waits on a transplant list.

This friend, Linsay, was twenty-eight when she was diagnosed,
and her hair has fallen out and grown back twice. With soft curls.
She's in remission now. The summer after my dad died, though,
she was placed on a list for a bone-marrow transplant. So she
asked that I donate blood and join the national registry, just to re-
plenish a stock she was sure to rely on while hospitalized. It was
the least I could do.

But Linsay needed me to hold off on the tattoo. She had been
an early coconspirator in its design, having weighed in on multiple
drafts. But, she explained, you cannot give blood for a year after
getting a tattoo. Giving blood now when she needed it, when she
asked, would be a symbolic act, meaningful for both how it revealed my obligation to her and for its potential literal end of sav-
ing a life, even if it wasn't hers. Waiting on this tattoo was the
small sacrifice I could make for her to communicate that I loved
her, that I would do anything I could to make this easier, to help
her think she was not nearly as alone as her cancer made her feel.
And I was willing to do whatever I could to make myself useful.

Of course I would postpone the tattoo until I could build up the
nerve to donate a pint of blood. That the donation and the tattoo
were linked in my mind drew out the process of nerve-building,
which amounted to several weeks of procrastinating, locating the
blood bank in downtown Brooklyn and the tattoo shop on the
Lower East Side, and deciding that I could handle the needles two
days in a row, that I could handle a permanent mark, that I could,
in fact, handle, if necessary, some doctor digging deep into my hip
with a boring tool to extract my marrow. Friends who saw me in
the days prior had no idea I was getting a tattoo, but they may never

forget how big a baby I was about donating that simple pint of blood.

The guy with the ink and the jar of petroleum jelly, the menacing man with the needle, wore sleeves of colorful, dangerous-looking, freaky tattoos—a massive pirate ship covering his upper arm, goblins, devils hopping about, and the bust of a humiliated Christ, crowned in thorns, on the other arm. He prepared his tattooing contraption quickly and methodically, hooking it up to its foot pedal, peeling away a sanitary wrapper from the needle, preparing for surgery. The machine buzzed in fits and starts before any actual work began, scolding like it was angry, reminding me this would be painful. Sitting there, staring at the ceiling, I was suddenly a young boy at the local barber sitting for my first haircut, the one you imagine will hurt, the one little children cry about because the scissors are so menacing.

All that is mine is yours, my stepfather had said. You have your mother. Take care of her, all of you. You have your siblings; take care of each other. And by his life of charity and compassion, no doubt inspired by Jesus, he continually says to me: You have the world I lived in, that Jesus lived in. You have your commandments—love God and love your neighbor. Take care of them.

And I never forget that all this came from a man whose body was ravaged by cancer, from a man whose father's body had also been ravaged by cancer. I saw the pain of it all on his face. Part of what he had, what his father had had, and what we shared with each other and with Jesus in our humanity, was this body—in health, vibrant yet balding, robust yet scarred; in sickness, jaundiced and frail, leaking bile from a hole in his gut, yet with hands capable of holding mine even on his last day, both of us exhausted from keeping him alive.

THE FAITH BETWEEN US

In the end, learning my inheritance through the early deaths of my fathers makes my life of faith all the more urgent. So I've gotten my tattoo. It burned a little. I have my fathers' initials—FJK and PAB—set in sharp, black ink on my right shoulder. And it reminds me to live.

Rather than suggesting permanence, tattoos prove our impermanence, our scarrability, the softness of our skin, the always vulnerable yet desperately held line between the quick and dead. Believing that the Christian inheritance is a worldly one while also knowing that a cab may not stop as I pass on my bike, or that I too may get cancer any day now, I am obliged to live and love as fully as possible. I believe in discipline, simplicity, and continually letting go. I believe in prayer, whereby I might see the world and my God in my neighbors, and encounter them always with compassion, hope, and love. Where Jesus always succeeded in this, I often fail. But I try hard not to.

Still, I bend toward God as I now believe God exists: as pure metaphor, the ultimate demand that I live well in the world. The Christian demand is to strive always and with humility for the ethical perfection exemplified in the life of Jesus, who in his weakness, powerlessness, and perfection actually was the Son of God.

And so here I am, scarred. I believe in God, in a way.

EPILOGUE
— PB —

For a long while I knew only one or two other people who had also lost a parent. It's a peculiar state of being, and after my mother died, I was often struck with a sense of terminal uniqueness. When I was in school there was always the kid who had lost a parent. We all secretly thought he was weird. Divorce, adoption, even a parent in jail paled before the kid who had a parent who had died. Among my friends and extended family, I was that kid following my mother's death. And strangely, this made me feel more Jewish than ever before, more religious, as if death was something peculiar to that state of being.

Death is the moment when everything is transformed and God becomes an actual force to contend with. When Job is standing amid the rubble that had become his life, he goes before God and demands some kind of explanation. "Though he slay me I will trust in him, but I will maintain my own ways before him," Job says. And God responds, perfectly describing the crushing weight of his ineffability: "Have you an arm like God, and can you thunder with a voice like this . . . Can you draw out Leviathan with a fishhook, or press down its tongue with a cord?" This is the God that was revealed to me when my mother took her last breath.

But then on a June morning in 2002, the e-mail arrived from Scott that his stepfather had died. Even though he had already lost his father years earlier, he was now an adult and had experienced death in close proximity, just as I had. Suddenly Scott was the weird kid also. The e-mail itself was short. All he said was that his stepfather had died, that he was glad to have been there when it happened, and that he was too tired to call and hoped I would not be offended by an e-mail relaying this news.

Later, as I reread the note after we'd finally talked about the night Paul died, I realized that Scott had lied. He had written, "My dad passed away last night. We were all around and he went peacefully." I now know that this isn't true. In our conversation, Scott told me he was out walking when his father died. Had I known then that he hadn't been perfectly honest with me in the note, I might have thought he was in a kind of shock when he'd written, and that he didn't really remember what happened, being so close to it, caught up in the swirl of so many people. But I know Scott better than that, and I know that he doesn't miss those kinds of details, no matter how traumatic, how devastating, how raw.

I think it's simply what he wished had happened. And what Scott ended up doing by projecting this idea out to me was create a narrative of the events that is less about the facts and more about the spiritual truth. So in one sense he lied, maybe feeling guilty about not being at his dad's side with the rest of his family, but in another he told the most real truth, that he actually was around his father when he died, as he should have been, no matter how far away he really was.

Looking back over it, I was also not surprised to see that Scott's e-mail didn't say anything about his hope for seeing his father again, either in heaven or at the Resurrection. I was not surprised that he, in fact, said very little about God at all, only thanking me for my "thoughts and prayers." And yet the idea of God was partly what defined our friendship, certainly part of why he decided to write me at all, and why, among all his friends, I was one of the first he told. But I didn't look for God in the things he said because I knew that, as far as he was concerned, the only way to see God in his life was in the things he did. What Scott didn't know was that I secretly envied all that he was slowly disavowing: the physical, concrete manifestations of Catholicism, the literalness of bodies and blood. My own faith can still be an often troubled, vulnerable thing that wants some form to cling to, even as I reject any idea of literalness. And yet Scott has always seen how this desire grips me.

There are nights when I pray to what seems like the emptiness, when all I can hear is the yowl of a dog begging to be let in. It is in these moments that I wish I had a form to focus on that might make more real an idea of God and the holy. Catholicism bursts with just such *reality*. Never mind the figure of a bleeding Christ on the cross, of a pierced and humiliated god; Catholics have all those angels and saints, a plethora of cosmic allies, waiting to hear their prayers. Why go to God, the invisible and unknowable, at all?

And yet Scott and I seem to agree that it's worth going to the source, worth attempting to dig into the depth of the human and find some language that might reveal some of this hidden God. We both love religious myth and find in these traditional stories the metaphors that reveal a way to talk about God, about spiritual encounters. But Scott also reminds me that how we talk about God is often beside the point. God is not something to be spoken about, but rather God is this demand that we live well in this world.

Scott made a graven image of his fathers' initials. But this isn't idolatry; it's where God really is, where his blood both makes a clot to bind the ink and promises Linsay, even if she can't use it herself, that life will continue to flow. Scott could have done as Matt charged and waited for a miracle, but we both know he would have waited for the rest of his life.

I wish God were the binding force in my friendship with Scott, but he's not. The thing that binds us, even stronger than the things we daily connect on—music, politics, his romantic dramas—is death. It's not merely that we have both lost a parent to cancer, a disease that changes all those who witness it, watching as resolve gives way to a slowly building hope and then to a sudden decline when all hope is drained away. It's not even that we both wrestled with the quality of our religious traditions in response to these deaths. We will both experience other losses, other terrible deaths and regrets, and occasionally tradition will simply have no bearing at all. No. What death has brought us each closer to understanding, by rubbing our noses in the mud of it, is that if God is not found in the world, he may as well be lost to heaven.

When my mother died, I was there. I watched her take her last breath, watched as my father cradled her body, listened as all of us in the room wailed and howled as though we were trying to scare her spirit right out of her. More likely we were yelling at God, feeling his presence more in that moment than in any other time in our lives. Here I was, as close to the divine as I had ever been, and God was taking my mother.

Afterward, and in a way Scott would never dream of, I went looking for signs that it meant something. And where I looked was in another place where I have often witnessed the sacred: in the spotting of a bird. And while most of my friends know that I'm a bird-watcher—Scott included—fewer of them know I believe in God. And then fewer still know that I turned to birds to find God in my life while I mourned for my mother. But to know why I love birds is to know what I believe about God, and to understand anything about my faith is to know why I love birds.

THE SNOW GEESE

— *PB* —

FROM A GREAT DISTANCE they first appear as a mile-long
ribbon floating on the wind. It is not clear what you are seeing, the
way they hover on the horizon. As they get closer, the ribbon
twists and bends, and you can begin to make out the density of it,
a thick black-and-white band fraying at the edges. Soon, but not
too soon, you can see individual geese, but for a long while it is still
mostly this crowded flock of motion. They circle the house once,
then twice, then still more, maybe half a dozen times. And then
the geese begin to descend.

It all happens quickly. When they are in the sky it's impossible
to tell how close they really are, but as they come down they seem
to appear suddenly, even though you have been watching them all
along. One by one they land in quick succession until all you can
see is geese. It's then that you realize, even after it has been going
on for minutes, that they are honking. The noise seems at first a
roar, until you realize you are able to make out the individual
honking of a thousand individual white geese.

It was the December after my mother died. I was in Maryland
for what was to be the second Christmas with my in-laws, and in
my lifetime it was maybe only the third time I had allowed myself
to be swept up in the holiday that, no matter its cultural impact,

was still like a foreign country. But here I was spending Christmas on a river in Maryland in a small white house surrounded by a flat expanse of farmland. If nothing else, at least there were birds. Since I've been bird-watching, of all the different birds I have seen, most of them I have seen on my mother-in-law's farm. Bald eagles, ospreys, and great blue herons live here alongside barn swallows, orioles, bluebirds, and turkey vultures. But on that Christmas it was snow geese.

When news got out that I had discovered the joy of bird-watching, that first year of holidays and my birthday were something of a disaster. Everyone gave me bird-related gifts: a plastic crow decoy, a bird marionette, wooden bird statues, books on birds, bird whistles, a clock that chimes out each hour with a different bird song, and assorted framed prints. Similarly, the Hanukkah after I started talking about taking on more Jewish observance, when everyone else was getting CDs and books I got a candle in the shape of a dreidl and a hideously large silver Star of David. Few people asked questions about the substance of my interest in either birds or religion. Friends and family simply treated them as private hobbies that they could support materially, but otherwise it was best to let me just do my thing by myself.

More often than not, I do bird-watch alone. But really it's usually more like bird-noticing. I am rarely able to carve out a special time to go looking for birds unless I'm on vacation or visiting friends or family who live rurally. So for the most part I am simply always looking for birds, while walking to work or taking a lunch outside. When I am with my son at the playground, I look for birds. When I am on the train to my father's house, I stare out the window and I look for birds.

Since I have begun bird-watching, my attention to things has changed. I listen more carefully. Sounds that used to be mere background noise have taken on greater significance. Without even realizing it, I am listening for bird sounds. Once certain bird-calls become familiar, you can recognize the bird they belong to more quickly. I have come to recognize that the sound of clicks and squeaky bicycle chains means there is a European starling nearby. If I hear a high and distant screech, all I have to do is look up to see a hawk circling. Even the common calls of crows and gulls have been pulled into the foreground. I can recognize wood-pecker hammering, cardinal chitting, and blue jay squawking. I also use my peripheral vision in a way I had not before, noticing the fluttering of a wing, the rustle of a branch, a shadow on the ground of something flying overhead. I notice these often ambient sounds and sights and then I look, actively look, for the bird.

I have spotted a surprising number of birds in Boston. I have seen boat-tailed grackles, Canada geese, cormorants, and mallards. In the early spring, terns nest along the banks of the Charles River. They stand perfectly still with the sharp black crest along their heads and their surprisingly large webbed feet. On the Mystic River, I have spotted kingfishers, bald eagles, coots, swans, and even a pair of merganser ducks with their balloon-shaped heads. In the urban areas between the rivers, on any given day I have seen crows, mourning doves, goldfinches, and red-tailed hawks. And, of course, pigeons.

Pigeons represent an interesting bird-watching conundrum. Before I became a bird-watcher, I had never really noticed pigeons, or at least never gave them much thought. They exist on the edge of one's perception. Maybe you have to nudge one gently out of the way as you walk into the subway. And everyone has fed a pigeon in a park. But to think of them as birds, to place them in the category of sightings I might check off on a list or in a field guide, well, at first I couldn't make pigeons a part of all that. But the more I started watching birds, my idea of pigeons began to shift. One morning, on my usual route to the Porter Square Red Line, I came upon a large flock of pigeons milling about. As I walked into their midst they quickly took to the air, and I saw, as if for the first time, that pigeons could fly. They have an impressive wingspan, and they are agile flyers. The flock broke up into smaller groups and landed in various places around me. I looked at them carefully, the variety of color, of size. There was a white pigeon speckled in brown, and a large bull of a pigeon, puffed up and cocky, looking for a mate. On that day pigeons became one of the many birds I observe, and I love them as much as any other.

In a mysterious passage in the book of Leviticus there is the story of Nadav and Avihu. The first section of Leviticus offers extremely detailed instructions for ritual sacrifice that culminate in Aaron, Moses' brother, performing an offering so that "God will appear to you." After a number of sacrifices, including a calf, goat, ox, and ram, God does indeed reveal himself to the people: "Fire came out from the Lord, and consumed the burnt offerings and the fat on the altar; and when the people saw it, they shouted and fell on their faces." In the next chapter, Aaron's sons try their hand at a sacrifice, but something goes terribly wrong:

> Aaron's sons, Nadav and Avihu, each took his fire pan,
> placed fire on it and then incense. They offered before God
> a strange fire that God had not instructed them. Fire came
> forth from before God and consumed them; they died
> before God.

There are a number of interesting modern commentaries on this passage, in particular one by Rabbi Yanki Tauber, who explains that Nadav and Avihu were not allowed to perform the same offering as their father, who was a high priest. But they loved God so much they attempted to get too close, closer than they were capable of (or merited), and were destroyed. There is another more mystical interpretation, this one by the celebrated Abraham Isaac Kook. Simply put, Kook explains that there are two types of spiritual realities. One is infinite, characterized by "pure awareness, like a flash of intuitive understanding," called chochma. The other realm, bina, is the chochma's finite shadow, where one experiences the pleasure of the spiritual experience, the bliss and ecstasy. But, of course, as a shadow, bina is the lesser spiritual experience. The chochma transcends even the greatest worldly pleasure. According to Kook, the two brothers mistook bina for chochma. They became attached to the pleasure of the ritual experience and failed to recognize the greater truth that existed beyond the mere offering.

I too once failed to recognize the greater truth beyond my own desire. Blissed out on drugs, I mistakenly believed I had found the key to enlightenment and a glimpse of the divine. I also got pretty badly burned. Because I was so desperately looking for something that God would never give me, I missed all the ways in which I might truly witness holiness, and it was here in the world all along.

I once saw a hawk flying inside a cloud of dozens of starlings. The whole of them moved in a twisting circle across the sky while the hawk tried to pluck one of the smaller birds from the flock. I had long ago imagined that if God appeared, it would be like this, with spectacle. Then, after much searching, I came to understand that God is often something so hidden that even with the patience of a bird-watcher, one might go a whole day, a whole week, without a sighting.

Recognizing God in what I had once considered mundane—the common pigeon and the cranky mockingbird picking on the neighbor's cat—took a deeper kind of patience I hadn't had before; not a patience of waiting, but a patience of tolerance, of letting things seemingly unrelated to God be the very place God can be found. Bird-watching has taught me this.

I was not accustomed to Christmas, and even less to such a rural place as this Maryland farm. It's nothing like what I knew of Christmases before I was married. I was far away from any city. Albino deer left tracks in the slush-free snow. And here, of course, there was a huge but tactfully decorated Christmas tree. And yet I relished in it. The dark, sweet smell of the fireplace, the presents, even the baked Alaska.

Christmas was something else before Amy and I started spending it together, before Sam was born. With everyone finally off the streets after the shopping of the last few months, it was nice to be able to walk down a sidewalk where everything was closed. Choices were simple: a cup of coffee, then a movie at the Brattle Theater, which always chooses something extra special on Christmas day—a Buster Keaton double feature, *The Godfather*, or *Sabrina*. And then, of course, Chinese food: a little fried fish in meat sauce, home-style tofu and vegetables, and hot-and-sour soup. Eventually I would be back at my apartment by myself. I'd watch *It's a Wonderful Life* and, grooving in the earnest treacle of that great film, I would in no way be aching for a table of relatives gathered around the ham. But more than that, the temperature of my Jewishness would rise as I welcomed not having to belong to anything on this day. My obligations were simpler somehow simply by *not* ordering pork lo mein at the Chinese joint and making sure I said the Shema, the core Jewish prayer that exclaims the oneness of God, before I went to bed.

But in Maryland I don't feel Jewish so much as I feel nebbishy. They have to make a special batch of mashed potatoes just for me (without milk), and I know everyone is wishing it was ham and not smoked turkey on the centerpiece of the Christmas dinner table. But on this Christmas, I was separated by an even deeper gulf. My mother had just died. While everyone was inside reading or napping, I took long walks around the farm. I tried to catch a glimpse of the pair of bald eagles that meditate on the frozen river. Sometimes, though, all I saw were buzzards, their huge wingspans like shrouds against the gray sky.

I first started really noticing birds on my way home to visit my parents when my mother was sick with cancer. Coming out of North Station and going over a small orange steel bridge that runs over the Mystic River, you can see gulls and cormorants from the left-side windows of the commuter rail that runs from Boston to Rockport. People in wheelchairs from the nearby rehab hospital are often there, alone or with their visitors, on a small deck overlooking the bridge and the river, where they can get some air or sneak a cigarette. The line runs into crumbling Chelsea and heads into crumbling Lynn with its beautiful brick and iron factory buildings. Between these two haunted cities the train rides past a protected wetland, and in the warmer months you can see egrets walking slowly along the banks. From Lynn, the train stops at Swampscott, Salem, Beverly, and beyond, following the coast. I disembark in Swampscott to visit home, just enough of a train ride to see the birds.

Most of the ride is monotonous scenery, so alike on so many

trains: the rears of buildings and parking lots, weedy hills covered by junk trees, and sometimes unexpected bodies of water. It's here that I first began to look for egrets.

At first I mistook these tall white birds for sticks or wooden markers, but as the train passed, suddenly their wings opened and they ran into the air, a spread of white so bright they seemed illuminated from within. After a few rides I became expert in spotting them, although I am often still tricked by a small branch standing upright in the water. Sometimes at a distance I can see half a dozen or so congregating on a patch of ground. It became a kind of game to spot them. I began to know exactly at what point on the journey to begin to look in earnest, pressing my face against the window. The wetlands end right at the General Electric plant in Lynn. If I saw the plant looming and hadn't yet seen an egret, I would feel a bit heartbroken. Once, I secretly wondered if this meant my mother had died while I was on the train. But the next ride out, there they were, lifting their heavy wings at the sound of the oncoming train, and I secretly felt relief. These kinds of thoughts began to take root and grow until I had a superstition that there was something connecting the egrets and my mother. This wasn't God's doing, surely, but in some way the fate of my mother and the egrets were linked. I began to dread the birds, because hidden in their existence was some truth about my mother's death.

There is a Yiddish story by Jonah Rosenfeld in which a man who is tending a sick goose finds himself in the barn on the night when the bird is struggling against its own death. The man had become increasingly fond of the bird and goes to it after he is awakened by the sound of beating wings. In the darkness, the old man tries to lift the bird and take it into his house to ease its passing, but the man loses his way in the dark. As the bird is dying, the man suddenly recognizes that he is not carrying a bird at all but the angel of death: "It isn't a goose he is carrying. It was a goose, but no longer is. It is a wing, only a wing . . . wings without a goose and with a weight that drags his arm. It is . . . death . . . death with wings, whose beating he had heard in his sleep." The man runs, the frantic dying goose fluttering all around him, until finally the beating of wings is something deep inside. The next morning, his daughter-in-law goes into the barn where she finds "the old man lying without a sign of life, and near him, without a sign of life . . . a goose."

A search for hidden significance seems to stem from a profound fear that there is no greater reality. It represents the greatest mistrust of God, the greatest kind of disbelief. It is idolatry in a way, believing that God is hidden in some earthly shape not as a prophet or messiah but in the forms of creation. This can even become a problem when considering the mystical idea of God as the *eyn sof*, the unknowable and the ineffable. From *eyn sof* come *sefirot*, or emanations, a tree of attributes from the topmost crown, *keter*, to the lowest form, *shekinah*, the presence of God in the world. God can only be known by these types within a taxonomy of the divine. The early kabbalists struggled with this conception of God and were accused of pantheism, the belief that God is in all things. If the *eyn sof* is unknowable, they asked, then how could God's emanations, the universe, as it were, not be equated with God? The implication became that God could only be known in the world, but that this is hidden knowledge, a religious secret. I have inherited something of this belief, and sometimes I can feel the spirit of something pulsing below the surface of things, as in the sighting of a bird.

I am always trying to interpret the world. This is a Jewish habit and one I happily accept, but it can sometimes get in the way of simply seeing the world not as any kind of reflection but as something real unto itself. But also, while I've rejected the superstition of reading the world as a code, as a Jew I can't give up interpretation completely. So I admit it. In trying to spot the egrets, or any bird, I am also looking for God. I know that God is there, I have seen signs of him, have heard the distant chirping, have witnessed his shadow fly across my life. But while I can notice God in the same way I notice birds, I can't *know* God in the same way I know birds. God cannot be captured in the merged vision of binoculars, cannot be measured and categorized as in a bird guide. (Even the Bible can't possibly get him exactly right.) Yet the attention that bird-watching has taught me, this I can bring to trying to know God.

But what, I have to ask, about the real bird, the flesh and feathers? The bird that is neither shadow nor symbol?

As a believer, I always get in trouble with myself (and with Scott) regarding the real bird. For example, the egrets that I look for out of the train window are perfect unto themselves, an evolutionary miracle, birds of prehistory, adapting, surviving, never "created" in the blink of an eye; at one time they were something else, something with scales and claws and teeth, maybe. It's easy to imagine these egrets as giants roaming those very same wetlands, feeding on now-extinct plants, themselves rising hundreds of feet out of the muddy waters. But when I spot one, there is something visceral I perceive as their creatureliness, their createdness. I can't go so far as to say these marvelous birds were "designed" by God, but I believe God must have had something to do with it. And yet here again arises the problem of language. Anything I attempt to say will be perceived as having some literal quality to it. But I'll go ahead anyway, because to describe our encounters with God, all we have are words.

One morning I was walking into the kitchen when I glanced out the window. Out on the neighbor's driveway there was an oddly large bird, particularly for the neighborhood I was living in at the time. I walked quietly to the open window to avoid scaring the bird away and saw what looked like a falcon eating something. I looked more closely and saw that between its talons the falcon had pinned a smaller bird, possibly a pigeon, and was carefully and precisely picking it to pieces. There were feathers scattered all around it, and every so often the falcon would cock its head, look around, and then continue feeding. It felt as though I had been given a gift, not only to see such a rare bird for the area, but more, to be able to watch it in all its birdness. I couldn't look away. There was nothing repulsive about what it was doing, even as I saw it pull the entrails up out of the pigeon's body and into its throat. I can only describe the feeling as ecstasy. Vladimir Nabokov describes this kind of ecstasy in his encounters with butterflies:

> It is a momentary vacuum into which rushes all that I love.
> A sense of oneness with sun and stone. A thrill of gratitude
> to whom it may concern—to the contrapuntal genius of
> human fate or to tender ghosts humoring a lucky mortal.

This is the God I believe in, this "whom it may concern" that is steward and spirit of the living world. When I see a bird, I understand something about God. In fact, the only thing I can really know about God is what I can perceive in the bird, in this kind of encounter. And so what does a bird reveal to me about God?

One day in the summer I gathered up my wife and son and we headed downtown. My son was two at the time, wide-eyed and babbling at all the people; he communes in perfect simplicity. We walked through the Boston Commons toward the Public Gardens to feed the ducks. At the entrance on the Charles Street side there is a brass statue, a mother duck followed by eight ducklings, in honor of Robert McCloskey's children's book *Make Way for Ducklings*. The actual ducks in the park are beloved by the city, and so other birds have found a home here, including Canada geese.

The geese have long sinewy necks, comical beaks, awkward but sure webbed feet. They are huge when they stand fully upright, and they can be downright mean. I looked at the geese in the Commons, threw them scraps of bread, and became astonished that they exist at all, that really anything exists, the miracle that there is something rather than nothing. And not only is there something, but there is such "a diversity of forms," as Darwin once wrote. At first three geese were eating, but then suddenly there were four, five, seven geese all around us. The abundance of birds, the magnitude of the things that exist, overwhelmed me. The geese hissed and twirled their neck around. They are fierce and surprisingly dangerous. There was peril here, of getting bitten, of being hurt. But the risk felt right as I stretched out my arm and let a goose take a piece of bread right from my hand. I could barely take it, the tension as the goose came forward and then grabbed the morsel of food, its beak sliding against my fingers.

God is the something rather than the nothing. God is abundance. God is diversity of form. God is dangerous and fierce. It is difficult to get too close, but the reward is that I can feel God slide against my life. The risk feels right. God "created" the world by being manifest in the things of the world. It's where he allows me to find him. But there is also the personal, the God that is present in my actual life, "my rock and redeemer."

On that particular day, as we made our way toward the pond, I watched my son waddle along in front of me and felt a thump in my stomach, realizing, finally and perfectly, that my mother never got to see him, and that he will never know her. I felt the slightly anxious murmurings, the awful doubt that, despite the encounters that I've had, God will not, or cannot, be personal in the way I long for. I try to imagine God and I either tumble into the nothingness or I cling to a superstitious set of principles that always fail me, always say nothing about what is real and needs attending to. As we continued to feed the birds, a giant goose got too close, and the three of us started moving back. Then I heard it. I heard in the chatter of the bird, in this absurd goose in the middle of the city, I heard the voice of God out of the bird's long neck. I threw bread at the goose, partly to distract it as it kept charging us and partly to attract it, to get as close to being bitten as I could stand. This is my faith, this repelling and moving deeper in.

There are times when all this active observance is exhausting. I am, like my faith, often lazy and distracted. I miss much of what there really is to see, and even in those moments when I know exactly what is required of me to have the experience I seek; when I might look into the branches of a tree just a little bit longer, I opt for the easy way out. But sometimes I find it is best to just let the birds come to me.

As when I scan the sky for birds, I look for meaning everywhere. It's a habit I have had to temper. But during that Christmas in Maryland it was hard to find meaning anywhere at all. I longed for the days when I thought the world was pulsing with hidden significance. The Jewish mystics understood this ache: "When Rabbi Abba saw a tree whose fruit turned into a bird and flew away, he wept and said: If men only knew to what these things alluded they would rend their garments down to their navels because this wisdom is now forgotten." I understand the instinct to look for hidden wisdom not in religious texts but in the natural world. In nature there are wonders all around, surprises in every tree, under every rock. As you drive along the dirt road toward my mother-in-law's house, there are two ancient massive maple trees that stand like sentinels keeping watch. It's hard not to imagine that these trees "allude to something," something that is now lost. It will never be found in a book or even a ritual. All that's left is the echo and the astonishing trees.

In Cynthia Ozick's story "The Pagan Rabbi," this quest for that lost wisdom is taken to its absurd conclusion. In it the learned rabbi Isaac Kornfeld has a love affair with a dryad, a tree spirit, in hopes of wresting from it the mystery of the animistic force he has come to believe resides in nature. But he knows that Jewish tradition forbids this knowledge. He believes that by coupling with the faerie, he will loose his own soul from its shell and be free to roam the world, unencumbered by the Law and tradition. But instead of his soul being freed, his body wrests itself from his soul and discovers his true soul to be forever bound by the Law: "He reads the Law and breathes the dust and doesn't see the flowers and won't heed the cricket spitting in the field." Kornfeld hangs himself, unable to reconcile what he desires and what he really is.

On Christmas Eve, when everyone had gone to bed, I snuck downstairs in front of the dying fire, the pops and cracks all that much louder for the silence in the house. There, alone, I put on my yarmulke and said the Jewish prayers before bedtime. I knew the geese were still outside. They would spend the night on the field and farmland, and when we woke we would all gather outside in the frosty morning to watch them take flight. I knew they were outside, the thousands of them, each a perfect reflection of the stars. It is written in the Zohar, "All the stars throughout the firmaments serve in this world, and they have all been appointed to have charge of every single thing that appertains to this world." But where is God, even when the upper and lower worlds so perfectly align?

The night was a hollow, empty thing. "He is my refuge and my fortress . . . ," I kept praying. "Into His hand I shall entrust my spirit when I go to sleep—and I shall awaken! With my spirit shall my body remain, the Lord is with me, I shall not fear." My mother was dead, my father was alone for the first time in over forty years, and there was a Christmas tree in front of me as I quietly said the Shema. I felt it again. God was absent. It was not that he did not exist. It was that God's presence in the world had been diminished. Had it always been this way?

But still I continued to pray and watched as my intent in the prayers began to change. I thought again of the geese. What if there were nothing but the geese? Were they enough to give me hope? If I had nothing else, if nothing else would ever matter again, could I simply find the idea of God in those birds? For a moment, lost and so far away from the city, I did. Was this not the hope of the golden calf, that the hidden and ineffable God could somehow be made visible, solid? I saw that God was in these birds, that I could know him in his creation. But then I realized that there was no magic to be found, no spirit of the bird with a message of life or death on its wings. And even though I fought against the wish that these geese were there for me, purposefully, deliberately, to give meaning to that night that was fraught with meaninglessness, I let myself believe that creation is only the shadow and that the real light is the hidden God inside the bird, calling to me from a secret place, emanating a reflection of his will in regard to my mother, to let me know that she is forever everywhere, even in the glorious honking of a bird.

EPILOGUE

— *SK* —

The first gift I ever gave Peter was a handmade ceramic mug featuring a rustic silhouette of a crow. No better than anyone else, I saw a material way to support Peter's interest in birds.

Visiting Jane's family over the holidays—we were still dating then—I mailed the mug, ostensibly my first effort at a Hanukkah present, from Portland, Maine, just a few days before Christmas, 2001. It was a piece of nostalgic, New England kitsch that, when I was a kid, my mother would have had sitting on a shelf in our downstairs bathroom, stinking with potpourri. From the same artisans' shop, in fact, I bought several other pieces by the potter who'd designed the crow stencil, only these were decorated with bears and moose, the motif my parents had settled on for their retirement home.

A few days later, Jane and I flew to Milwaukee for what would be my family's first Christmas at that cabin in the middle of rural Wisconsin. We all knew it would also be my stepfather's last. From now on my mom would be spending most of the holidays on her own every year. I thought of Peter's father, alone again in Swampscott, his son making the long trek out to a Maryland farm with his young family to see the snow geese. While my dad was still around for my mom, this year it was important to all of us that she have something to remember.

And so on Christmas Eve we sat longer around the table at dinner; we prayed longer at Mass; we had more drinks and let the fire burn longer into the night before heading to bed. (My dad, sick, was long asleep in his chair.) Then, Christmas morning, we lingered longer opening gifts around the tree. We made an extra pot of coffee. We passed around an extra batch of cookies. It was all just the same, but there was more of it. So it felt strange. I handed over one of the gifts I'd brought with me from Maine, and my parents appreciated it much, much more than a ceramic butter dish ever actually deserves.

When Peter called later in the day to wish everyone a happy holiday, he could sense before I said anything at all that this Christmas was turning out to be something like the one he'd had that first year in Maryland: that is, it felt like a foreign country. Before we got off the phone he politely thanked me for the gift.

"I love it," he lied.

Now, in all my visits in the years since then, I can't say that I've ever seen my mug in Peter's kitchen cupboards. I've certainly never drunk from it. Maybe he's stashed it away with the massive Star of David, his bird puppets and whistles, and the dreidl candle, bound up in a box under his bed next to the clarinet. The clock that announces each hour with a particular birdcall still hangs above the door to his pantry, though—perhaps simply because it's practical to have a clock in the kitchen. Sam's probably learned to like the sounds it makes too. Or maybe the clock mimics the sounds so accurately that it's actually taught Peter a thing or two about that ritual of bird-watching; maybe it's helped to make the voice of the European starling or cardinal as familiar as the voice of his son or the face of his mother. Sam's always underfoot, always talking. And scattered throughout the house are a few small photographs of Peter's mom, Ruth, each one more glamorous than the next. It's simple. Peter's filled his home with reminders of those awesome encounters he's had with God. It's been impossible not to, I suppose. God shows up just about everywhere we find life and death.

Though he might not use the word himself, of the two of us it

can be said that Peter has always been the more faithful environmentalist. More than I tend to, Peter often describes the world as
God's creation. As such, it deserves our love and protection. His
reflections on birds reveal a tendency to amplify, just slightly, the
natural world, with the divinity that sounds quietly—almost
imperceptibly—behind everything. So Peter can describe God not
just in the tremendous migration of snow geese over his mother-
in-law's Maryland farm, but also in the awful urban falcon greed-
ily devouring a pigeon on his driveway. From this perspective,
God is real and signs of him are everywhere.

And while I don't disagree that faithful people can—and really
must—talk meaningfully about God's will and our obligations to
one another through metaphors drawn from the natural world, I
haven't ever found anything particularly holy in a pigeon, especially, say, one left for dead in the bicycle lane. Crushed by a cab
Monday morning, by Tuesday it's been picked apart by its canni-
balistic brothers. As I pedal by, if the poor guy says anything at all
from the other side, it's only to wish me a little better luck in traffic.

But then again, there may be something holy even in that, in
that wish that I be careful, that I take my life—living itself,
really—seriously. After all, if dying fathers can remind me of the
value of life, perhaps, if seen from the right perspective—if properly watched and *noticed*—this dead bird might remind me just as
well. In his faith, Peter tells me that like any other creature, I live.
And like any other creature, I'll die. So will he. My mother will.
My whole family. Everyone.

Ruth did. My fathers did.

But they all lived too.

Calling this fact part of God's creation—yet not going so far
as to call it his plan or his design—makes meaning of our very
creatureliness. I may not, as Peter does, ever describe God as dan-

gerous or fierce; I may no longer imagine a creator behind this creation. But my religious tendency now is to show how obviously meaningful our lives can and should be. We share with the rest of nature a place in the life cycle, a world of joy and suffering, broken wings, broken hearts, and broken bodies. Still, the cycle we share is about living.

And for most of my life this was the last thing I wanted to admit about myself. Far from sharing much at all with the natural world, I considered belief in God—often a fierce and dangerous one—the thing that set me apart entirely from nature and from other people, too. Of course, this is the story I tell of accepting a religious calling as a teen and keeping a vow of celibacy through my mid-twenties. I transformed a facial tic into a moral compass. Yet over the years, nothing has set me apart more, nor engendered such an unnatural—and as I saw it, perfect—relationship to the world, than my approach to food. What's more natural, after all, than eating? How could *I* ever eat like other people eat? As with everything else, it seems, God had simply made me too good for that.

THE VEGAN

— *SK* —

AH, SHIT, MONDAY hit me hard. And normally I liked Mondays. It was seven-thirty a.m., late October 2005. I'd overslept by two hours and missed an early train to D.C., where I was expected for a noon meeting with the archivist at St. Luke's Episcopal Church. As usual, I ran out of the house without eating.

I slept in fits on the train—hungover and woozy the morning after a date—my mind racing with excuses and apologies for both the church lady and my friend David, whom I'd arranged to travel with. Not surprisingly, his phone calls from my doorstep at 6:00, 6:05, and 6:07 hadn't roused me, and he'd had to leave me behind. When we'd made plans over the phone around ten the night before, just as the wine was served before my meal, he wasn't convinced I'd be awake in time. By three thirty, when I said good-bye and declined Alycia's offer to stay the night—*I still have to pack; I'm leaving in a few hours*—she wasn't convinced either.

Sure, sure, she'd said.

I'll be back in a few days.

On the train, angling my cap to keep the sun from punishing me, it all flooded back, and it hurt. I'd collapsed into bed without packing when I got home, not entirely sure how I'd gotten there. I pieced together my long walk. My alarm hadn't worked in the morning. There'd been no time for a shower. I smelled. In my panic—I hated being late—I'd thrown some things into a bag, forgotten my deodorant, I realized, and stumbled out the door.

I hadn't been convincing about much of anything on the date. Mostly we talked about food. She loved Indian and we'd never be able to eat that together. She'd traveled and had always eaten what was set in front of her. I was choosy. Disciplined. *Sure, sure*, she'd said.

With her, especially where eating was concerned, I'd been un-convincing for as long as we'd known each other. Without an en-vironmentalist or animal-rights angle, my veganism—no meat, no dairy, no fish, no eggs, in other words, my individual cheeseless pizza that night—made no sense. And she let me know it.

"What if *you're* traveling and a family invites *you* for dinner?" she'd said. "Tell me again: You dated a pastry chef for almost a year—*you slept with her, right?*—and you wouldn't eat a pastry? What's wrong with you?"

At the moment—my boozy head swimming in regrets while, over the phone, my professional apologies to the secretary at St. Luke's sounded unsteady—apparently a lot was wrong. I left an apologetic message for David, too, and hoped he'd still meet me for dinner someplace. *Wherever*, I said. I'd never eaten in Wash-ington before, but after four years avoiding most foods, I'd gotten so that I could find something to eat on just about any menu.

About fifteen minutes out of D.C., I called Peter on his lunch break and managed to fill him in on the night I'd had—a success-ful date, I said; "Good," he murmured, unconvinced—without saying anything at all about food. See, even after all these years, having faced together the death of my stepdad and his brother's suicide, even after sharing Sabbath dinners with his family—when his son once asked, "Is Scott a person of us?"—at least one thing in Peter's and my shared life of faith had gone unsaid. I'd always passed on the challah because I knew it contained eggs. On the next night, we'd have the same problem ordering in from a local Indian place. I passed on most of it because of the clarified butter. I'd become a religious eater, and those ingredients were against my religion. I had come to say that I was as disciplined about eating as I was because it made me disciplined in how I approached the world. And I had mostly come to believe it. Admittedly, even at the time it strained the logic of my religious imagination. I'd already given up on the reality of miracles. Yet I saw veganism as an ethical commitment in the Christian model of "love your neighbor as you love yourself," where asceticism was a kind of self-love that could teach me magically to love my neighbor.

When we recited the prayers in Hebrew and toasted with kosher wine, or in Peter's case, grape juice, as a Catholic I'd had no trouble at all. What made the eggs in the Jewish bread so different to a vegan? If I could pray with him, why couldn't I eat with him?

Like everyone else I couldn't eat with, Peter had always seemed to buy my logic around food, or at least never let on that he didn't. (I'm sure many people have seen right through me and have been kind or uncomfortable enough not to embarrass me by pressing.) Yes, even I'd mostly bought it by now.

That date before my trip to D.C. was successful at one thing, that's for sure. It got me thinking about eating again. I'd started doubting myself while dating the pastry chef the previous year, but never let on. I continued the self-doubt at wedding receptions that summer, where it was difficult to eat. But I ended my phone call with Peter without saying any of this. *Why start now?* I thought. He started to tell me about the weekend and his sister-in-law

Sarah's wedding. "Call me back later, will you, Peter? I have to go," I said. "I'm pulling into the station."

Of the two of us, Peter has always had a more loving, less complicated or fearful, relationship with food. While most of us have food issues, his seem mild. As he gets older, he's more careful about fats and bad cholesterol. He no longer drinks, of course, and increasingly he eats in a "kosher style." Yet the ritual meals he celebrates with friends and family recall his mother's brisket and her delicate gestures over the shabbat candles more than they invoke strict dietary laws that distinguish between sacred and profane foods. He'd like to share with his son not just the practice of prayer but also the joy of eating as a Jew. Peter's eating habits are rooted in Jewish tradition. Eating itself, apart from providing basic sustenance, is more nostalgic than superstitious, and what passes his lips only rarely intersects with what food historian Felipe Fernández-Armesto calls the "foodways which belong to the sphere of the sacred."

In my family, there was never any joy of eating as a Catholic. There was religious eating, of course, and prayers specifically about food. Food was God's gift, given from his bounty. We received it. Or alternately we abstained from it: No meat on Fridays during Lent. There were even days leading up to Easter when we fasted altogether. But the reasons for this—to feel hunger, to taste a kind of suffering—were mostly lost on me. As usual, religious practice was not important for what it might have taught me about the way others lived and struggled. As far as I was concerned, fasting was just another deed that individual Catholics did to get to heaven. Abstaining from certain foods—like abstaining from sex—kept the believer in God's good graces.

Seen from one perspective, the Gospels are all about food. Jesus' first miracle is to turn water into wine during the wedding feast at Cana. Jesus' first disciples, including Simon Peter, whom Jesus would choose to head his church, are fishermen. Jesus first impresses them with a miraculous catch, filling their "boats so full that they began to sink." The most famous New Testament miracle is the hillside feeding, by Matthew's account, of four thousand people "besides women and children" with seven loaves of bread and a few small fish. The leftovers alone fill seven baskets. And then there is the miracle of the upper room. On the first day of Passover, Jesus sends two disciples into the city where, just as he said they would, the two encounter a man carrying a jar of water. The man leads them to a house where the upstairs guest room is already "furnished and ready" for Passover, the Last Supper.

Of all the church's rites and traditions, the sacrament of the Eucharist, or Holy Communion, which is based on the words Jesus speaks while sharing bread and wine with his disciples in that upstairs room—*This is my body . . . This is my blood*—is central and the most vital to the faith. Food is at the center of Catholicism. But the belief that something magical happens both in the priest's preparation of the bread and wine (that they become Jesus' real flesh and blood) and in our receiving them (that we come into direct contact with the Savior), made the experience for me as a child entirely about personal salvation. Like the cannibals we supposedly were—receiving flesh and blood—we believed that, as Fernández-Armesto writes, eating "affects the eater." The greatest hope for faithful Catholics—a hope shared with actual cannibals— was that Communion would "burnish their characters, extend their powers, prolong their lives." Eternal life could be found in a wafer and a sip of wine.

But the food was never good. The drink was always as cheap as the church could find. Which is how it seemed it should be, after all: After fasting for forty days in the desert—another New Testament food miracle—Jesus was tempted by Satan: "If you are the Son of God, command this stone to become bread." To which Jesus replied, drawing on the book of Deuteronomy, "Man shall not live by bread alone." There is more to life than eating. Something so trivial as taste could not matter if what was really at issue in eating religiously was the spiritual effect of what we were given to eat. And ultimately, if it was more beneficial to the soul to resist every one of the devil's tempting offers than to indulge—from a piece of bread while fasting to premarital sex—then the answer seemed obvious. Jesus was clear: Abstaining is good for you. Celibacy keeps you pure. *Not* eating affects the eater as much or more than eating does.

In Washington's Union Station, options for food were everywhere. Something for everyone: The Corner Bakery Café, Center Café, East Street Café, Cookie Café, and Café Renée. Cajun Grill, Wingmaster's Grill, Station Grill, Thunder Grill, and Uno Chicago Grill. A New York Deli. McDonald's, of course. Sit-down places called America and Acropolis. A carry-out Soup in the City.

There was Nothing But Donuts.

But there wasn't time. The archivist was waiting for me at the church. I had no idea where I was going or how to get there. I was late enough as it was. Most of these places were fast, but I hated fast, and more, I couldn't stand to eat on the run.

So I just ran. The station was jammed with commuters eating. I bumped against them with my luggage. I hailed a cab outside and slid in.

"Fifteenth Street and Church," I said, and we pulled away.

I closed my eyes again. There was something in there for

everyone—but me. Again, not eating was nothing new. And something to be proud of, I thought for a very long time.

Just as I really began not having sex when the opportunity presented itself on the floor of my girlfriend's bedroom at fourteen, I began not eating just as soon as I could as well. In my household, preparing dinner was an after-school chore, something I usually started in the hour before my mother got home from work. And as a chore, I enjoyed it. I watched cooking shows on TV during the afternoons to hone my skills. And supper was on the table when my dad arrived.

We were midwesterners with midwestern habits and diets. A corn-fed, meat-and-potatoes family like most of our neighbors, we drove places more than we walked places, ate a fair amount of fast food, and exercised irregularly if at all. So we carried some extra weight, some of us more than others. Though by no means obese—or particularly unhealthy as an eater, I think—my stepdad was the heaviest.

And as with most of my big decision-making then, responding to fear (in this case, of food), vanity (thinking skinny is more attractive), and a sense of my chosenness (experienced over and over through disciplines of self-sacrifice), I decided I would be different.

Vegetarianism was my method, beginning at seventeen, of becoming and staying slim. And it worked. I helped prepare meat dishes (sometimes meat-stuffed-meat dishes) for my family and ate the vegetable sides. But there were also salads without dressings and breads without butter. No fast food. No desserts. No more breakfasts. Nothing I ate tasted particularly good, so I didn't eat very much of it. (I still eat only twice a day.) I often stepped onto the bathroom scale, pleased with the low one-twenties—I was once more than twenty pounds heavier—and dropped into the high one-teens at my thinnest. I was cold most of the time. I did a thousand sit-ups every day for years. I thanked people when they said it was clear I'd lost weight. (No one said I looked good, just thin.) I told my parents not to worry when they heard the same thing from the neighbors. Of course they worried anyway.

Coinciding, though perhaps not coincidentally, with my most serious considerations of joining the priesthood, this discipline became a compulsion when that vocation burned out.

But what I called "vegetarianism" I've recently recognized in the anorexia among the Catholic nuns described in Karen Armstrong's memoir *The Spiral Staircase*. Like Armstrong's convent sister Rebecca, and Armstrong herself, I nearly proved that man not only shall not, but actually cannot, live by bread alone.

Armstrong's book, subtitled *My Climb Out of Darkness,* is an account of her "escape" from an English convent where she failed to find God ("I did not believe that God existed . . . and wondered if I ever really had") and also describes her dealings with panic attacks and the onset of epilepsy, both of which were eventually stabilized. For Armstrong, religious devotion and asceticism were expressed through a strict control of money (her rationale for starving herself) as much as food: "I, however, was choosing of my own free will not to eat. I was often ravenously hungry, and would sometimes allow myself a piece of real toast and butter, which, if I had been truly anorexic, I told myself, would have been quite impossible . . . My purpose was, I believed, simple and pragmatic: I wanted to save money . . . If I built up a reserve fund . . . I would be set up for life and could eat and spend whatever I wanted." Her conclusion, of course, is the one I can offer only now, with hindsight: "I made it sound rational, at least to myself, but this was a crazy scheme and a telling indication of the state I was in." In time, Armstrong got psychiatric help, and in dealing with her seizures took the appropriate medications.

I just got worse. Being thin was a horrible, embarrassing rationale, worse than money. I knew it as vanity, a weakness in me, and nothing I could ever say out loud. So I called my fear of food "vegetarianism." And for a while, that was enough. People assume a lot about you when you say you're a vegetarian: You love animals. You're an environmentalist. You want to be "healthy" (which is what I said, mostly). In fact, I was as much a health-foodie tree-hugger as Armstrong was a holy miser.

This went on for eight years, from seventeen to twenty-five, and in time my weight—like Armstrong's panic attacks—stabilized. But my obsession grew worse. Knowing that the rationale of "health" was not enough, I had to change my reasons for not eating. Like Armstrong, a fellow Catholic, I had gone so far in controlling my diet because I wanted to be transformed. At a certain point, my body had become sufficiently thin. Yet as Rebecca says in *The Spiral Staircase*, "I wanted to be another kind of person." As always, still the best. And certainly better than I was.

I sought what could be called perfect eating. Or, again, *not* eating. Asceticism was an actual religious discipline; fasting was holy. And so, without my really realizing it as it happened, the disciplines of not eating became religious. My devotion to the Eucharist—the literal body of Christ and the path to salvation—shaped my approach to all food. I began believing in discipline for discipline's sake. I abstained from sex. I abstained from food. I was better for both, more like Christ. And for a time, vegetarianism was good enough.

Until I lost my virginity, at least.

Jane was a vegan. No meat, no dairy, no fish, no eggs. The timing works out, although I can't say that it presented itself this way to me at the time. But just as it seems no coincidence that I became a vegetarian around the time my priestly vocation faded away, it's no surprise that I took on another food discipline just as I gave up my vow of celibacy. In giving up one religious discipline, I needed another to take its place. Less scared of sex, I became more scared of food. Already most of the way there—I already feared most food—I began eating like Jane simply by giving up the daily cups of yogurt and reading the backs of packages hoping not to find whey listed among the ingredients. Once the rhyme of *"Good, better, best . . . ,"* my mantra now became another cliché: We should eat to live, not live to eat.

At St. Luke's, after hunting for the entrance I was greeted by a seventy-five-year-old woman who playfully scolded me for being late with a school-matronly gesture of *Put up your dukes, son.* I bowed a little instead. Embarrassed and still woozy—by now starving, too—I would have taken a dive had she really swung. Just one solid punch would have done it. I'd have deserved it, too.

"I'm so sorry I'm so late," I said. "My travel was delayed." Just delayed; she didn't need the details.

I explained my work as an editor of a documentary edition of the papers—letters, diaries, newspaper writing—of a former slave named Harriet Jacobs. My host sat with me at a card table I was sure she'd struggled to set up while waiting for me, and watched as I leafed through newspaper clippings and old sermons written by renowned black minister Alexander Crummell, the founder of St. Luke's. The archives were small for so historic a church, I thought; but I was grateful my business there would be brief. Researching Harriet Jacobs's church life, I quickly turned up her name in a membership list from Crummell's congregation between 1873 and 1883, the first decade of the church. That was all they had. I was done. My schoolmarm gave me a quick tour of the chapel and sent me on my way by two thirty with directions to my lodgings and another display of fisticuffs.

Now what?

It was hours before I could check into my hotel. I'd never toured the capital before. I went looking for someplace to eat among the monuments, memorials, the White House, and museums. But nothing seemed right. Block after block, my mind continued to race. When I couldn't find anything, I realized it was because I just couldn't bring myself to eat. There was something wrong with me. Something had to change. Maybe I'd been vegan long enough, I thought. Maybe too long.

Eating with Jane had been so easy. Never so many choices. Never so hard as the night before. Never so many questions. Never that kind of defensiveness.

Veganism was good for Jane and me in the same way sex had been. It brought us together as often as twice a day to share a meal together—often from the same plate. With her, eating took on a social character I hadn't known since I started picking around foods at my family's dinner table and preparing my own meals in particular contrast not only to what, but also to when, everyone else was eating. Over time, eating had become an almost entirely private ritual—as embarrassing and holy, I guess, as weighing myself every day, or those lonely moments Peter spent scraping pot resin from the bottom of a bowl. Before her I'd mostly eaten alone, arranging my mealtimes to avoid family suppers, eating something before I went to a dinner party so I wouldn't have to face what was put before me. Food kept me apart.

But with Jane, who seemed equally scared of food and just as private, we had favorite restaurants and favorite supermarkets. She became my partner around the stove and the table as much as in bed. Strangely, food itself almost became good again. I started to care about how things tasted.

But then again, with both of us so fearful, this was almost no better. Dinner for two, even with a certain variety, can be just as lonely as dinner for one. Only now, with company in my loneliness, I began to see in someone else my own embarrassing and irrational fears. And when the relationship ended—several times over several years, and ultimately not until she met someone else she planned to marry—my old habits returned. Meals became rote.

For a time, huge bowls of granola and rice milk, filled to the same line each day, supported me from morning until evening even as I biked often twenty miles a day—another habit I picked up from Jane. Even the accoutrements of food had their place in my new rituals. In another daily fit of undiagnosed obsessive compulsion, I would buy a cup of lentil soup and a bagel for lunch, but then would have to measure between two fingers the thickness of my stack of napkins before I could even start eating. Yet I stopped ritual fasting on Catholic holy days after blacking out on an uptown train the morning after Ash Wednesday one year. Commuting with my roommate, he dragged me to a subway police station at Columbus Circle, where I sat for twenty minutes with my head between my legs. A nurse at the clinic thought it was low blood sugar. After that, I also gave up the tradition of giving things up during Lent; my life had become one big discipline already.

It's no wonder I so often refused to eat with people, and actually a little surprising people weren't more often refusing to eat with me. Holiday meals with my family were more work than they should have been, and I could always hear the disappointment in someone's voice after I'd recommended we have dinner at another vegan place. There is also the sense that when you eat with a vegan, he is always silently judging you. Suddenly, though,

I was beginning to feel that censure in reverse. Although it had been some time since I'd measured a stack of napkins—this ritual very quickly made me feel nuts—on this trip to Washington, I was, more than ever, a very strange and defensive eater.

If the discipline was supposed to make me better around people, why had not eating suddenly felt so unconvincing on my date last night? And why had I felt so comfortable and confident making people so uncomfortable? How much good can a discipline do if it keeps you from eating what a loved one prepares for you?

That didn't matter. We should eat to live, not live to eat, I repeated.

Yet as much as ever, this discipline—much as I had come to understand all the others—had meant I was still more or less scared to live.

I was on Pennsylvania Avenue, about a quarter mile from the Capitol in the distance, when David called, offering tourist advice and more directions to my hotel. I'd been wandering around a few hours, I said. "Really sorry for missing you this morning." "No, I haven't really seen anything." "Yes, St. Luke's had what I needed." "No, I haven't found a lunch place." "Dinner later? Sure. I'm starving. Good."

He'd meet me at nine with some friends at an aviation-themed restaurant called Café Saint-Ex, named for Antoine de Saint-Exupery, the French writer of *The Little Prince* and books about aviators.

"See you then. Fourteenth and T Streets."

In the meantime I'd try to find something to tide me over, I said. But in fact I never did. I traipsed around more, still not really seeing anything, then found my hotel and changed clothes. The woman who checked me in suggested a few places for food near

the Howard University campus—I'd said anything would be fine—
and then mentioned she'd serve breakfast in the morning, starting
at seven. The other guests might join me.

Thanking her, I headed back out for more wandering.

I arrived early to Café Saint-Ex and sat at the bar with a scotch
and soda. A propeller hung on the wall. The waitstaff wore T-shirts
with airplanes on them. Without anything in my stomach, the
scotch hit quickly.

I looked over the menu. Organic greens. I could eat around a
goat cheese croquette, I decided. Soup of the day was made with
local organic vegetables. The wild mushroom risotto was made
with red wine and fresh herbs. Or I could make a dinner of sides,
$4 each:

> Smoky Lentils
> Wood Grilled Greens with Lemon and Garlic
> Brussels Sprouts with Balsamic Vinegar and Pine Nuts
> Organic Sweet Potato Puree

"Are all of these vegan?" I asked.

As expected, Peter called just before nine, so I stepped outside and
perched atop a newspaper box to hear the story of his sister-in-
law's wedding. Sarah and Carrie looked beautiful, he said. Sam
had danced with Amy. The food was wonderful. A bartender,
though, had accidentally served him a cranberry drink with a little
vodka, which, after a healthy sip, threatened his seventeen-year sobriety. It wasn't exactly a technicality.

No. I realized as we talked that Peter's sobriety, as a practice of
faithful discipline, had made that entire day possible for him. I
was reminded of something Amy had once told me soon after

Sam was born: Sobriety is what makes Peter's marriage possible. It allows him to be a loving father. It binds him to Amy and Sam and now to this growing family: That day he'd welcomed a new sister-in-law. His own faithfulness is reflected in every dance between his wife and his son. It's reflected in his friendship with me.

Veganism, as much a discipline as sobriety, had never been so faithful. It had made nothing possible. Ultimately it bound me to no one.

David arrived with his friends a little after nine, and I waved them on ahead of me without interrupting Peter. I'd join them in a minute. "Peter," I said, "it's been a really difficult day. I haven't eaten a thing. I just couldn't. After my meeting at the church this afternoon—seriously, I just walked. All day. Let me call you back tomorrow. My friends are here. I'm meeting them for dinner."

I don't believe it was Catholicism or religious belief itself that had misserved me for all those years where food was concerned. No priest had ever recommended I drop below a hundred and twenty pounds. No bit of scripture prescribes with any precision how thick a stack of napkins should be before a diner can take his first spoonful of soup. No, as with anything in need of interpretation, it was my approach to the faith—as much with my *faithful* approaches to vocations and sex and bodily purity—that had kept me aloof and disordered my eating. It may be true that all of what I had found in religious eating is there to be discovered in the Scriptures and Catholic rituals and tradition. This is particularly true where Catholics, like certain, mainly literalist, Christians everywhere, stress piety and personal salvation over concern and engagement with the community. Yet in an essay titled "Onward, Christian Liberals," Marilynne Robinson remarks that this focus on "personal holiness" is not supported even by the most prolific, and arguably the most influential of the early Christians—more influential even than Jesus in shaping the church. "[Personal holiness] suggests a regime of pious behaviors whose object is the advantage of one's own soul. It suggests also a sense of security concerning final things, which is understood as a virtue, though it is in fact a confidence not claimed even by the Apostle Paul."

Veganism was just such a pious regime. Yet just as Robinson reminds us that Paul's biblical writings are concerned mainly with building communities of humble and loving Christians, the Gospels seem equally unconcerned with individual piety or holiness. Where food is concerned, nowhere in the Gospels do we find Jesus eating alone. The food miracles at Cana, on the Sea of Galilee with the fishermen, on the hillside with the four thousand hungry believers, and in the upper room with the twelve disciples are all about serving other people, dining together, sharing food and breaking bread. Where eating actually serves the individual soul, to borrow another phrase from Robinson, it involves an "openness to the perception of the holy in existence itself and, above all, in one another." True holiness is evident in the Gospels when Jesus makes it possible for people all to eat the same fish, bread, and wine. And because miracles are mythical evidence of the presence of the sacred in the world (or, more simply, the sacredness *of* the world), the quality (or quantity) of what the miracles produce is important. The wine Jesus produces in Cana is the best that is served all evening. And as for the bread and fishes, there is not just enough, but with God, always an abundance: more leftovers than they even started with, enough fish to sink a boat.

I've been leading up to this, but as we approach the end let me put something plainly. It's important. Technically, I've become an atheist.

Again, my early doubts about the reality of miracles and my

broadly metaphoric reading of the Bible have now led me to understand God himself—miracle of all miracles—in completely metaphoric terms. This makes it difficult, but not impossible, to remain Catholic. After all, I've always had a religious imagination and continue to develop my spiritual attitudes.

Where Communion is concerned, though, since I no longer believe that bread and wine become body and blood of Christ on the altar, I am arguably more Protestant in my belief than Catholic. Holy Communion is a metaphor. Nothing magical happens when we eat in church. Still, Fernández-Armesto is right: Eating may affect the eater. But just as I no longer believe in the facts of the miracles from the Scriptures, I no longer believe that "there are substances you consume to make yourself holy or intimate with the gods or ghosts." Not as a Catholic. And not as a vegan. Food magic has done me no good.

In *The Year of Magical Thinking*, Joan Didion's meditation on the death of her husband, the novelist and screenwriter John Gregory Dunne, she recounts a point of religious contention between the couple that had lasted forty years. Like me, Dunne was a Catholic who, at a point, stopped believing in the resurrection of the dead and did not find great literal meaning in Holy Communion. Yet his approach to the Eucharist was Catholic in the same way mine has become. Didion recalls, " 'Only Episcopalians "take" communion,' he had corrected me one last time as we left St. Sulpice . . . Episcopalians 'took,' Catholics 'received.' It was, he explained each time, a difference in attitude."

If there are not any personal gods or ghosts to become intimate with, religious eating becomes less pious and, actually, more biblical, more about serving others. Without any connection to actual spirits—as we've seen before with regard to the great value of religious myths—what becomes important to religious eaters are the *spiritual attitudes* we form about food as an essential part of living and a building block of a holy existence. It's no longer a matter only of what we eat, or what we believe we're eating, but how we eat, and why.

Given the right spiritual attitude, every meal eaten with others can be a religious meal. Blessings and prayers of thanksgiving said before meals remind us both of our dependence on others and on the natural world—God's creation in both cases—for the food we eat and the joy possible in finding more moments for communion with friends, family, and even strangers. Given the right spiritual attitude—say, that the eater has truly *received* the meal he sets before himself—even eating alone can be a religious experience.

The absence of such experiences, as a scared vegetarian and later as an apparently terrified vegan, has taught me the value of food. And yes, given the right approach to food, even fasting can prove valuable again for precisely the reasons I'd missed as a young Catholic. People starve. And with this new approach to food, Jesus loses his power as the otherworldly ascetic starving himself for his own sake, as I had attempted. As we read in Paul's Second Letter to the Corinthians, he stands as the model of compassion: "For you know the generous act of our Lord Jesus Christ, that though he was rich, yet for your sakes he became poor, so that by his poverty you might become rich." Whether the generous act is understood as God's becoming human or Jesus' living among the poorest of the poor—and demanding of his fishermen friends that they do the same—the message is no different. And forever I was wrong.

There is no perfect eating. There is no perfect not eating. There is only eating or not. When you have an opportunity to eat with or feed other people, take that opportunity. When you have the chance to fast in a way that will remind you of the poverty of others or your own poorness of spirit, fast.

Go for Indian. And when you love a pastry chef, eat what she sets before you. Even if, on occasion, there is nothing but donuts.

I found David, his girlfriend, and their friend already seated on the patio. David had ordered olives for the table. Introductions were made. We had drinks all around. I spent a little time with the menu again: Organic greens. Vegan sides. The goat cheese croquette made me nervous. Risotto.

When the waiter arrived at the table, he looked to me and I froze: "Start with me last," I said, pointing to David. I ran my finger down the list again: Smoky lentils, wood-grilled greens with lemon and garlic, brussels sprouts with balsamic vinegar and pine nuts, organic sweet potato puree. Four dollars each, I thought. I ate an olive.

David ordered a burger. I ate another olive. His girlfriend chose the risotto. Coming around too fast, the woman next to me ordered the organic greens, seven dollars, and house smoked-salmon sandwich with goat cheese, tomato, and mixed greens. Nine dollars.

No one else knew what was coming. And no one else cared. The waiter looked to me.

"I'll have what she's having."

And it was good.

EPILOGUE
— PB —

One of the first times that my wife and I had someone join us for a Sabbath meal and the kiddush blessing was when Scott was visiting from New York. It was only the second time we had met in person. But what to serve? What to serve? At the time, Scott couldn't even eat the challah because it was made with egg. Amy and I decided on some cooked lentils and salad. Scott passed on the bread as it went around. But as we gathered at the table for the blessings, I realized what we were having for dinner didn't matter. We had found something we could all eat, and that was enough to sustain us.

Saying kiddush with my wife and son in front of Scott, I felt free. I wasn't worried that I would have to explain what I thought about the words or what I believed about them. We gathered around the table and I poured some kosher grape juice into a cup almost to overflowing: "God blessed the seventh day and set it apart. For on it God had ceased from all the work that had been done in carrying out Creation." Raising the cup, a brass goblet that belonged to my mother, I said first in Hebrew and then in English, "Blessed are you, the boundless one, our God, the sovereign of all words, who creates the fruit of the vine." What we all shared in this moment was gratitude for the things we have, for grapes and their juice, and for family and friends to share it with. And for language that gives all this some expression.

What does it mean to say aloud that God created the world in seven days, to bless that moment as if it happened in real time, to give thanks for it, but to not actually believe it? The Jewish theologian Rabbi Arthur Green asks this same question much more succinctly in his book *Seek My Face*: "How can I *affirm* that which I do not *believe?*" As I passed the cup to Scott to drink, I passed the other truth of this moment, that which I can affirm. Language is a vessel, like the cup, and what it holds is the juice, but not the fruit. The prayer contains the sweetness of the story, but the pulp and the rind are things we must put in the compost heap of history to let the years slowly decompose, to be used again, to grow new grapes, so that we can drink again.

It's interesting to see these objects in relation to their counterparts in Catholicism. For Jews, blessing wine during kiddush does not turn it into something else. Instead, the blessing draws attention to the metaphor of the wine—how it represents sustenance, abundance—and anticipates the literal drinking, making greater meaning of the way it tastes, the way it quenches thirst. In the ritual, the wine's literal force—as actual sustenance—gains metaphorical significance. It becomes more meaningful than it really is, which is not possible if literal wine were to become another literal substance, like blood.

Ritual and tradition provide substance for the metaphors we find in myth. They give form to the poetry that often leaves you merely haunted. Here is the wine: Please recognize its marvelousness before you drink it. Even though Scott couldn't eat the bread, we could still say the blessing over it together. Here is the bread: Please give thanks before you eat it.

Like many of Scott's friends, I relied on his asceticism as a moral compass. His celibacy was the idealized sex life, his veganism the idealized eating life; even his tic represents a kind of worldly imperfection that he'd taken as proof of an otherworldly perfection. For Scott, each ethical decision is existential, is *important*. And while this might be an impossible standard to try to match—much less for him to live up to—it's certainly one that is a guiding light. And the foundation for all of this was a belief in God. Or so we all thought.

But I knew his veganism couldn't last. For one thing, all his friends are such foodies. There are only so many variations of baby greens that one can find in even the best restaurants around New York. But more important, I could sense that it was keeping him from really being in communion with others in the way that he aspired to be. To be both the most popular and the odd man out was an agonizing tension. He was the coach in the wheelchair, urging everyone around him to play their best and embrace their lives while he sat on the sideline with a megaphone and a whistle. And then, as I expected it would, the phone call came.

Scott ate meat.

And even though I was not completely surprised, it still hit me hard, because I also knew when his veganism went, along with this celibacy, something else had to give too.

Scott's an atheist.

I knew it was coming to this also. For a long, long time. But I didn't know if I could bear it. I don't know what hit me harder. Was it trying to imagine Scott eating a plate of ribs, his face and hands greasy with barbecue sauce, and afterward using a toothpick and making sucking noises to get the bits of flesh out of his teeth? Or was it knowing that now there was a gulf between us—with Scott, the one person I could tell without hesitation that I believe in God, that I believe there is an ultimate reality. Did I suddenly have to be embarrassed about this around him? It had always kind of bothered me that when he visited we could never really share a meal, that I couldn't amaze him with my chicken soup. But at that moment I was hoping he would go back to his hummus sandwiches if it meant he might believe in God again.

As each thing is shaved away, what remains? What I found, after my initial scare, is a more thoughtful faith, one that relies not on the possibility of any actual transcendence but on the most human values. And despite some pretty serious theological differences, it is truly faith that we share. I didn't know it, but this had revealed itself already in that first meal Scott and I shared. These days I am happy we can eat more together. But I am happier we can, despite his disbelief, still pray together.

THE PRAYER BOOK

— *PB* —

NOT LONG AFTER MY SON, Samuel, was born, I found myself in front of Grand Opening. Located far enough away from
the Combat Zone, Boston's version of a red-light district, it's become known as the place where fashionable people buy their
videos and vibrators. I had come from Cambridge to Brookline to
buy a siddur, a prayer book, but I was stalling. In Grand Opening
I would at least have an idea of what all the fuss was about: I knew
about sex and had a newborn to prove it. I would be less sure of
myself in the Jewish bookstore down the block.

Regarding my son, Sam, there were more than a few perplex-
ing issues. The first was that Amy is not Jewish. And strict Jewish
law defines descent matrilineally. There was also something vaguely
bothersome about the quality of his circumcision, which seemed
to have left a little more of the foreskin than I thought it should.
And I am still more than a little superstitious. I was worried that if
circumcision really mattered in some metaphysical reality, this one
was not going to cut it. But my anxiety over my son's circumcision
or his Jewishness is not so much about him, or God even, than it is
about my own relationship to faith, to God, and to prayer.

If I had run into someone I knew on the way to buy a prayer
book, I probably would have said I was going to Brookline to do

some shopping, mentioning the comic book store, the independent bookstore, or even the bagel shop, all three good alibis among people who know me. Who wouldn't go out of his way for a dozen excellent bagels? The sex shop could have been as likely a destination, and among friends, easier to swallow. Given the choice between sex and prayer, well, if you put me up against a wall, I'd more readily admit to visiting the sex shop. I am only a little embarrassed about going into stores like Grand Opening, which is owned and run by women. I am much more embarrassed about going to buy a prayer book.

Sadly, Brookline is the only place in greater Boston to get something like a siddur. It is the last remaining Jewish enclave in a city once filled with them. From Chelsea to Dorchester, Boston was once made up of a number of Jewish neighborhoods. My father grew up in Roxbury before his family and others eventually found their way to the suburbs to avoid increasing crime and decreasing property value. While there were, and still are, Jewish areas outside of Boston, this was the end of the truly urban immigrant Jewish communities. For my father's family, however, the suburbs lacked urban character and access to things like museums and delicatessens that he and his parents had become accustomed to, so Brookline beckoned. Many Jews set up shop and stayed. All I know of this earlier Jewish world are the stories my father tells me, of him walking a mile from his neighborhood to sneak a Hershey's bar on Passover, chasing the ice trucks in the summer, and eating pickles right from the barrels on the sidewalk. Yet the butcher, baker, funeral home, and kosher deli he talked about—they're all still there today. So when I went looking for a prayer book, I knew to head to Brookline.

I stepped off the subway into a warm spring downpour, and as I walked across the street to Harvard Avenue, I looked back at the train as it squealed away down Beacon Street. The Boston Green Line is slow and crowded and there aren't nearly enough trains to meet the demand of commuters. But they run along the street, *outside*. Once they go above ground, they get their power from their pantographs kissing the cables strung above the avenue. The street is completely wired all the way down the center, but I've grown so accustomed to the cables that they no longer register.

As I began to walk toward the Jewish bookstore, I noticed that the comic shop was advertising a fifty-percent-off sale on back issues. I had time so I stepped inside. I knew I belonged in that store even more than in the Jewish bookshop. I belong to that world of comics as much as anyone else. I know more about the Marvel and DC universes, have more trivial knowledge about the Fantastic Four and the Avengers, than all the philosophy and theology I studied in graduate school. At my regular comics shop in Cambridge I have been a customer for well over twenty years. Inside the Brookline store I browsed the cardboard bins. The names were all so familiar. It's a language I know intimately: *Legion of Super Heroes, Daredevil, Thor, Swamp Thing, Doom Patrol.* I was able to move through the sale items quickly. Like anyone in his thirties or forties who is still reading comics, I can sometimes recognize a title merely from the font of the first letter, can tell by a cover price approximately what year the issue came out. It's like being immersed in Talmud.

Comic books don't make me feel awkward in the way religion can. That's not to say that as an adult I haven't been embarrassed about reading superhero comics. Once I ran into a colleague in a comic store and we acted as if we had bumped into each other in a strip club. My instinct was to make myself appear as though I was just browsing until I knew whether he, too, was a serious collector. Yet when friends come over for dinner, I don't bother to put away my stack of *Justice League of America*. I do, however, hide my yarmulke in the top dresser drawer.

Nevertheless, I don't feel the same kind of responsibility to comics that I feel to God. That day, however, my belief in God was starting to feel like the damp sweater I was wearing. I could chat with these guys about the new issue of *Hellboy* and feel cool. But knowing I was on my way to buy a prayer book, I felt like a schlub. I felt old. My son was at home with my wife, my umbrella was barely functional, there was a hole in the bottom of my shoe, and despite the rain I was sweating. I left the comics store empty-handed.

Outside was the wondrous Coolidge Corner Theatre. The marquee was filled with the names of films you couldn't see anywhere else in this city. I felt a tug toward it, toward the sanctuary of the movie house, air conditioning, a cup of coffee and a bag of popcorn, alone in the center, ten rows from the screen. I began to falter in my original mission. To buy a prayer book is to commit to a set of particular words, particular ideas, be it Jewish or otherwise. Simply to believe in God does not obligate me to say any one thing about God. But once I begin to pray with some liturgical language, I become enmeshed in those words. Words, particularly religious words, so easily become concrete. Words are a way of containing the ineffable, that which, in moments of real religious reverence, feels beyond language. Any attempt to name it would be to limit it to those particular ideas. But more often than not we latch on to these ideas and the vessel becomes the very thing it was intending simply to hold. Words themselves become icons.

How is it that the most natural religious instinct to give form and shape to the divine is also the most dangerous, both personally and culturally? The Bible itself tries to counter this impulse. In

Exodus, Moses tells the Hebrews that God has asked that they make no graven images. Not long after, Moses goes back up to talk with God, and the people get a little restless. Aaron, Moses' brother, tells everyone to melt down all their gold and fashion it into a calf, a common image for the divine in the ancient world. When Moses sees what they have done, he is angry at them for breaking one of the first commandments they were given. But who doesn't feel sympathy for the Hebrews, doing only the most human thing, to try to give form to the holy, to the ineffable? But the commandment stands for a reason. To worship God in the image of a calf threatens eventually to reduce the enormous reality of God to the much smaller reality of the idol.

Similarly, after Solomon builds God's temple, he looks around and says, "But will God indeed dwell on the earth? Even heaven and the highest heaven cannot contain you, much less this house that I have built!" Literal interpretation is the same as trying to put God into a house that a human being built. It's inauthentic and dangerous because it moves us further and further from a relationship with God that is tremulous, doubt-ridden, terrifying, and exhilarating. After all, how could an experience of something so far beyond our grasp possibly leave us calm, cool, and collected? If God is great, encounters with God should sometimes shake our very being. Literalism also imposes limits on God, suggesting that what is infinite can be assigned finite categories.

With regard to prayer, the question is: Should we accept the literal meaning of the words, or do we try to reimagine their meaning in a way that conforms more to our own experiences and situation? If we accept the literal meaning of the words we find in prayers, then we are not doing what Martin Buber, for example, calls true religiosity, which is to take religious ideas and "imbue them with new and incandescent meaning." A relationship to religious language that is literal makes us feel too safe, too stable, and too fixed.

This is the strange paradox, for example, of literalist readings of the book of Genesis. In this reading of nature, God created the world in six days, and on the seventh he rested, almost six thousand years ago. From here God quickly set in motion how it will all end. The younger the planet is, the sooner it might all be over. From this perspective, what seems *really* terrifying and more unbelievable are the billions of years it took to really get things going. In *this* extremely old world, the messiah—the hope of Jews and Christians—could be a long, long way off. Better to believe you at least have a shot at seeing it happen. In a world as young as six thousand years old, every generation has a chance. The trouble, it seems, is a fear of oblivion—a long, dark, and meaningless sleep. Infinity is lonely, and we all want to cling to finitude, stability. Let eternity come when we are safe in the arms of God, not helplessly waiting in a chaotic world filled with unknowables and uncertainties.

The saddest thing about reading Genesis literally is to become blind to its story. It's in story where what is holy about language is revealed, just as music reveals what can be holy about sound. To read Genesis literally is to learn a series of facts. There is no engagement or dialogue. Stories and myths are how we construct a narrative of the holy, a way of giving language to that which is beyond language. It is only when we engage in a kind of conversation with our myths that they become alive. Metaphor, other figures of speech, allusion—these are the human vessels that we mold. Metaphor is where we wrestle most authentically with God, in the shaping of God into story. The failure, always, is making an idol of the finished clay pot, the statue. If it's taken at its word, the living text is reduced to an object. God demands this of me, not to make an idol, not to carve an idea of God into stone.

Literalism removes our sense of the mystery, where we are with God in fear and trembling, what philosopher Søren Kierkegaard describes as our true relationship with the divine. To approach God in this way, without certainty, is hopeful; it takes the pressure off us to have to know perfectly what God is. A Jewish prayer for the end of the day reads, "Tremble and sin not, reflect in your hearts while up on your bed and be utterly silent. Selah." Be silent. If only in those few minutes before you fall asleep. Enough with all the talking and the naming. Enough with all the idol-making. My own fear in approaching the Jewish language of my new prayer book was that any words I used to speak about or to God were idols, and I was intent on smashing them.

The one store where you hope for a discreet entrance has a snappy spring bell on the door, loud enough to alert my father in the suburbs. On my right were magazines, videos, books, and to the left were the toys. And by toys, I mean dildos. Shelf after shelf of dildos. Dildos shaped like cats, dildos shaped like rabbits. I walked over to the videos, head down. Any trace of confidence, self-respect, or a righteous indignation that *by all means I was going to do what I wanted to do when I wanted to do it*, all of it was left out on the sidewalk, slowly making its way down the sewer with the rainwater. Any feeling of longing or fantasy that had fueled my coming here in the first place had evaporated. I was now the creepy balding guy in the old clothes delicately fondling the video boxes. While I stood there, a group of young college-age girls walked in, right past me and over to the dildos, and began to laugh riotously, snatching up the silicone toys, trading them back and forth, bending them, laughing some more. I simpered at the clerk at the counter, a woman about my age, and fled out the door, the jangling bell announcing my exit. I raced down Harvard Avenue.

I finally arrived in front of the Jewish bookstore, but before going in I decided I could use something to eat, so I stopped at the only kosher delicatessen for miles around. Boston was once filled with them, but as the Jews left for the suburbs and more and more gentiles started to like Jewishcentric cuisine, there was no more need for the kind of strict regulations to keep a kitchen kosher. For a moment it felt as though a nice kosher meal was the only thing I really needed to be close to God. Something so simple, to eat and be nourished, can make me feel closer to God than prayer. Everything about it is holy: that we are provided for, and that what provides us with life can give so much pleasure. To be sustained, and this sustenance should feel so good. Why worry about the afterlife?

I often built my identity as a Jew around my family meals when I was growing up: brisket with kasha, lox and whitefish, corned beef, pastrami, potato knishes, and matzo ball soup. The first time I ever ate dinner at a friend's house his mother placed before me a plate of macaroni and cheese, tuna fish, and carrots, each in its own little ice-cream-scoop pile. I didn't know what to do, had never seen tuna fish outside its home on slices of rye bread; had never, ever seen macaroni and cheese. To be polite, I ate the tuna, and it tasted *empty*. At the deli, I ordered pastrami on rye, a side of stuffed cabbage, a plate of pickles, and a large Coke. An eternity without spicy yellow mustard? Forget it.

After lunch I went into the bookstore, pastrami on my breath. I was still not sure if this was where I belonged. Prayer was about words and language, and words are religion's biggest problem. But I was desperate for some formal expression that felt both ancient and relevant to my life, a life of interfaith marriage, the

Justice League of America, and a son with a slightly skewed circumcision.

On my shelf at home there are a number of different siddurs. One set belonged to my parents, *The Union Prayer Book*, a polite, mostly English version from the Reform sect of Judaism. I never once saw my parents take it down off their shelf, rarely saw them go to synagogue at all since I had been born. We sat as a family to eat during Passover and Rosh Hashanah, and my dad told plenty of Jewish jokes. But the prayer book stayed on the shelf.

I also have a worn and tattered prayer book that belonged to my maternal grandfather, which he took with him overseas during World War I. His name is written on the inside front cover, Willie Sorgman, in what I imagine was his eighteen-year-old scrawl. The book looks like it was used. Maybe he really did pray three times a day, as prescribed by Jewish law, in the foxhole. If so, I wonder what his gentile fellow soldiers thought of that.

In my early twenties, right after I got clean and sober, I excitedly became more observant of Jewish law, keeping mildly kosher, trying to relearn the Hebrew left over from my bar mitzvah. I spent some time at a local Chabad house, and was given, along with a beautiful and already much used set of phylacteries—also known as teffilin, the leather boxes observant Jewish men bind to their head and upper arm, containing the prayer known as the Shema, the pivotal declaration of one God—an orthodox prayer book. I used it, along with the teffilin, for a few months. And then I stopped. I had tried to take on too much too fast, and I became disenchanted. I continued to pray in my own way, mostly in private, sometimes at a local synagogue on the High Holidays. I still kept "kosher style": no pork, no shellfish, no cheese on my hamburger. I went on like this for some time, feeling vaguely satisfied with my religious life—something that didn't make much demand on me, and I little on it.

Then I watched my mother die in the arms of my father six short weeks after her diagnosis.

It was as though the very roof of the house were torn off, and God descended to take her. There is a Jewish superstition that if there is no way for the soul of a person to leave the place where she died, that soul will be trapped. With the roof gone, her soul was sure to get away. (To be safe, several years later I made sure to open a window in the room where she passed away, just for a minute. Just in case.) After my mother died, my belief in God was shaken so badly I began to have anxiety attacks. Real panic. When I slept I would wake every hour, the feeling like someone sitting on my chest. Exhausted, I would fall back asleep and then wake again, feeling afraid of death. And there was no God anywhere.

A dear friend and rabbi suggested a series of prayers known as the Bedtime Shema, and she pointed out a version found in the *Artscroll Siddur*, the traditional orthodox prayer book, with Hebrew on one side, an English translation on the other, and plenty of commentary. I prayed these prayers every night through terrible bouts of anxiety in the wake of my mother's death, pushing my way back toward God, back toward the possibility of meaning in the face of mortality. I eventually got there.

A year later, my son's birth was not unlike the moment of my mother's death. There was a lot of wailing, a lot of fear of both the known and the unknown, and when he finally arrived, after hours and hours of labor, the roof was again ripped off. God descended once more to change everything in my life, utterly, forever. But I didn't respond with panic and anxiety as I had when my mother died. I responded with a question. What will God really be in my life and in the life of my family? I was hoping some kind of formal prayer would give me the answer. So I went to

Brookline to find another prayer book, not a hand-me-down, but finally one that I picked out myself.

I took from the bookstore shelf the prayer book I was after, my palms sweating, my desire a flutter in my belly. I flipped the gilded pages, my eyes quickly scanning the words, looking to see how a particular one was rendered: Did it press itself onto my idea of God, or would I have to press back to it, making the words translate into what I believe, what I so desperately wanted God to be? The shop was hushed; but I still felt self-conscious. I paid for the book, fumbling with my wallet, and walked out. The door silently closed at my heel.

After seven years of marriage, I still quickly pretend I'm doing something else if my wife walks into the room and catches me praying. It's an instinct I can't quite shake. But at the same time I believe a prayer life is central to a life of faith, that there must be time in each day set aside for things that are not about parenting, being a husband, sex, music, or, of course, comic books. Yet prayer is really about all these things, because they are what I return to. I don't have to make a choice. The language of prayer doesn't commit me to thinking or believing one thing about God. Prayer is simply the dialect of my faith.

There are two things about my prayer life that are inherently Jewish. The first is that I have a prayer life at all, and that I have designated time each day for it. I pray in the morning, short personal prayers and then the Shema. I wait until my wife is in the shower and then I close the bedroom door and pray at the foot of my bed. At night, when everyone is asleep, I take a little more care. Again I say a series of personal prayers, for myself and for the well-being of my family. I try to recount where in the day I fell short of what I believed I should have done. I list my sins, and I ask for forgiveness. And then I say the bedtime collection of prayers I learned after my mother died. These are no longer the prayers of anxiety and restlessness. They are the prayers of closing a day in thanksgiving and in awe.

Nevertheless, the quality of my prayer is sometimes lacking. On the subway, walking down the street, if I suddenly feel worried, I don't always remember that I can stop and pray. It is important that I carve out a time to pray each day, that I can look forward to it. But setting aside a time for prayer also partitions prayer in one's life, and often, as with faith, prevents it from being brought fully into the world. And then there is doubt, as much of a companion as faith.

Sometimes when I pray, all I can sense is emptiness, a nagging doubt that what I am doing is absurd, that there is no dialogue to be had because there isn't any God. I am sitting on the couch with my prayer book and my yarmulke and I might as well be talking to my son's Batman doll on the floor. But I keep at it, because I know that my formal prayers are really just warming up for a real life of faith, where what I do will count for much more than what I say.

As much as I distrust religious language, it still provides the best metaphors we have to talk about God. I believe that God is something that I can be in real relation with, and that in some way we can know God, if only with the faulty language we have access to. I believe that transcendent truth exists, that there's something beyond human relationships and the natural world. I continue to look for this truth, but also try to find God in the here and now. Judaism insists that God loves the world and its works: "When you eat the labor of your hands, you are praiseworthy and it is well with you."

In particular it's the Psalms that offer a religious language that seems the most human and worldly. Their yearnings, their dreams, their sorrows, and their reverences are so embedded in the human experience, it's impossible not to be moved by them, even if you don't believe in God. They are the words that clarify our own longings:

> *O God, you are my God, I seek you,*
> *my soul thirsts for you,*
> *as in a dry and weary land*
> *where there is no water.* (Psalm 63)

> *For all our days pass away under your wrath;*
> *our years come to an end like a sigh.*
> *The days of our life are seventy years,*
> *or perhaps eighty, if we are strong;*
> *even then their span is only toil and trouble;*
> *they are soon gone, and we fly away.* (Psalm 90)

> *Praise him with trumpet sound;*
> *praise him with lute and harp!*
> *Praise him with tambourine and dance;*
> *praise him with strings and pipe!*
> *Praise him with clanging cymbals;*
> *praise him with loud clashing cymbals!* (Psalm 150)

The Psalms are not God's words, but ours. They are not laws, prophecy, or even letters. They don't even presuppose anyone will read them. Sometimes they are painful to read. There is violence and despair. And there is faithfulness sometimes blind in its veneration. But I know what that is like. It's the same reason I went looking for a prayer book. I believe. I believe.

I believe what the psalmist believed, that I have had an encounter. If you ask me if I believe in God I'll tell you yes, but I can't tell you anything about God. I can only tell you about these encounters. God reveals himself to me in the world, in relationships, in death, in birth, in watching a hawk above the city, its call audible even among the din of the traffic. But those grand metaphors still hold. For when I watched my mother die, I understood the psalmist when he wrote, "The voice of the Lord causes the oaks to whirl and strips the forest bare; and in his temple all say, 'Glory!'"

A life of prayer, of daily prayer, is dangerous, because metaphorical language—mythic language—can begin to feel commonplace. It takes effort to reimagine the words as you say them. Combining prayer with meditation allows you to have a different kind of focus on the words, and allows the meaning of the prayers to unravel and take on different shapes. Prayer will not draw God down. Prayer isn't a magic spell that will make things happen or make God appear. Prayer is the clothing for the encounter, the garment that illuminates the invisible features. Prayer shows off God's figure, as it were.

In my family life and my life of faith, there will be some ritual and the breaking of bread. I can give my son some semblance of a Jewish home. As for seeking God, Sam will be left to go the way I did, in uncertainty and doubt, and hopefully with a little bit of wonder. But when the time is right I'll have a prayer book for him, I hope worn and dog-eared by then.

EPILOGUE
— *SK* —

Those nights are long gone when I would ask an angelic switchboard operator to patch me through to heaven. In fact, except when they come to mind involuntarily like all-time favorite pop songs, I've more or less stopped saying personal prayers. The transition's been slow. Since those early, comforting nights improvising prayers that always began with *"My dear Lord God"* and ended with the affirmation *"Amen"*—meaning basically *"Yes, I believe you can do anything"*—I've run the gamut. Long ago I'd memorized all the traditional prayers. Poring over the Scriptures and reciting from prayer books, I've directed my reading to heaven. I've repeated at home the petitions from Mass known as the Prayer of the Faithful: for the needs of the church, for the world, for those in need, for my own little town. *Lord, have mercy.* Hymns have kept me awake. God heard it all.

Nowadays, though, the Father isn't there to listen to me silently meditate on the Lord's Prayer, and the Holy Mother doesn't intercede with her Son each time I call her to mind with a Hail Mary. I'd always really understood church petitions to be prayers for miracles. Now outside of its context within a community able to act on it, a prayer asking God to care for the poor floats away unheard. Kept to myself, any prayer for the sick is just as ineffectual.

It's not just that I've imagined the human connection with God and his heavenly hosts has *changed*. With no actual, personal God to connect with, I can't believe anymore that any real connection between heaven and earth exists at all. For me, the question that arises around the sort of daily personal prayer that Peter practices is not rooted in the doubt that goes along with knowing God to be too far beyond our reach for us ever to encounter him. No, if my trouble with God were mere doubt, I'd still pray to him. I'd long for the encounter Peter believes in. I'd have a personal God and call out as a true New Testament believer, "Lord, I believe! Help my disbelief!"

But I don't. After all, there's no reason to pray if there is no encounter to hope for, if there is nothing out there to help me, if God doesn't actually exist. It's no longer enough for the Lord to have mercy. I've come to believe that *we* must.

So it's not doubt but belief itself that stands between Peter and me. It's as simple as saying that he believes in God and I don't. He's the theist, and I'm the atheist.

And not that he—or anyone—needs my approval to carry on a personal prayer life, but even from my perspective, his commitment to daily devotions is *ultimately* meaningful. For a man whose wild, impatient, and superstitious pursuit of God almost killed him, nothing could be more faithful, nor inspired, than Peter's calm practice and his discipline of daily prayer. On the other hand, for a man whose discipline, supposedly in the service of God, kept him really from loving and performing God's will (and also almost killed him), the last thing I need is another daily practice to make me feel chosen. No, Peter and I don't need the same life of faith. What we need—and perhaps what we all need if we're willing to consider the will of God—is to look at the life we do have and find ways to make it always more faithful. We are called, by God and each other, to fulfill our obligations to our family, friends, and neighbors—and as the Christian myth encourages, even strangers and our enemies—always more perfectly.

While not at all interested in whether I thought God might have created the world in six days, or if he had actually performed any of the other miracles we both knew from the Bible, when

Peter first asked if I believed, he wanted to know whether I'd ever encountered the holy. Had I met God the way he had? Had I trembled? And then, even as I answered *Yes*, even while I still believed in a personal relationship with God, the efficacy of prayer, the miracles of the Eucharist and the Resurrection, eternal life, heaven and hell, even then our connection was not in our experiences of the holy but in our very decision to talk about God. No, I had not trembled. No, God had never torn the roof off my life. God was never so violent. God was never so powerful. Instead, God had always had my life safely under his control. In short, we connected then in our shared belief in the basic value of religious language and the power of stories to make meaning of humanity's encounters with the sacred.

"Yes," I said, "I believe." And that was the breakthrough. We started to explore faith together. Through what we thought was a shared belief in God, though, we learned to believe in each other.

Today, however, after years of friendship, we face a new and perhaps bigger question: Is belief itself, the belief we thought we shared, actually irrelevant? Is the hope of encountering God even necessarily at the heart of a faithful life? Can a Jewish theist and Catholic atheist really share a faith between them?

I say again, Yes.

Peter and I still speak the same language. We can both talk of God's Creation without my having to believe that there ever was a Creator. With God as pure metaphor, I can faithfully and religiously care for God's Creation by living *as if* he were behind it all. We can both talk of the will of God without my having to believe in God himself. I can faithfully and religiously do his will by living *as if* there were a God. Belief, as Peter says, is irrelevant. What matters is love.

It's as true from a Christian perspective as it is from a Jewish one. Jesus imagined a better world. In Luke's version of the central Christian teachings known as the beatitudes, Jesus preaches that the poor will be blessed. The hungry will be filled. The weeping will laugh.

Even at our most optimistic, we rarely if ever sound so hopeful as this. That's because Jesus believes in love more than we do—although not, I believe, more than we *can*. He would never ask more from us than is humanly possible.

Yes, in a strange biblical twist, by placing his ultimate faith in us, in Jesus, God acts *as if* there is no God. He challenges us to do the difficult things. To bless the poor. To feed the hungry. To comfort the distressed. Love God and love your neighbor, he says, and then he goes away. He dies as one of the poor, the hungry, and the distressed.

Dietrich Bonhoeffer has written of this approach to Christian faith:

> The God who lets us live in the world without the working
> hypothesis of God is the God before whom we stand
> continually. Before God and with God we live without
> God. God lets himself be pushed out of the world on to the
> cross. He is weak and powerless in the world, and that is
> precisely the way, the only way, in which he is with us and
> helps us.

And so, in this way—before God, with God, and without God—I pray with a devotion I share with Peter:

My dear Lord God, may God help us. Amen.

ACKNOWLEDGMENTS

This book has been the result of a series of remarkable and serendipitous events, all of these set in motion by some remarkable people. Together the authors would like to thank the most important of these, our agent Jennifer Joel, who saw us through quite a ride to get here. But it was Kathy Belden, our editor, who urged us to be the best writers we can be, and whose firm guidance helped us bring it all home. Thanks to Stephen J. Dubner for being an integral part of the story we tell here. Thanks to Karen Rinaldi, Colin Dickerman, and all the folks at Bloomsbury USA. We also want to offer our sincerest thanks to Paul Elie for seeing something in our initial pages, and whose suggestions were ultimately to provide shape to our narratives. And finally, thanks to Don Cutler for suggesting we tell our own stories in the first place.

Scott would first like to thank all his family and friends for their endless and unconditional support over the years spent writing this book. Thank you to Roger Hodge at *Harper's* and Darra Goldstein at *Gastronomica* for their wise and graceful edits on pieces of this book that first appeared in their magazines; to Rabbi Leon A. Morris for his faithful guidance through Jewish thought and ethics; to M. Ryan Purdy and Whitney Pastorek for their friendship and creative collaboration in the world of self-publishing; to Matt

Laufer, Ben Rutter, Melissa Lang, Joel Blecha, and Deanna Pacelli for helping me think and for reading various drafts along the way; and to Father Ned Coughlin, SJ, for inspiring me to be the Catholic I've become. Many thanks, of course, to Peter and his family for inviting me to be, as his son put it, "a person of us"—that is, family. Special thanks go to my brother, Frank, and my sister, Sara, for all their love, and to my mother for everything and more. I write in loving memory of my fathers Frank Korb and Paul Boglitsch.

Peter wants to thank all his family and friends for being such a loving community. Special thanks to Rabbi Devon Lerner for being a confidant and a friend, and to Patrick Doherty for spiritual advice. Thanks to Joe Gallo and Jason Patch for being all around mensches; to Stefan and Ruth Economou for support and cakes; to Melissa Glenn Haber for writerly discourse. Also thanks to Emily Neill, Sarah Neill, and Judy Ashworth for giving me a second family; to Bob and Jim Neill; to my big sisters Karen and Lisa for all your love and hopes for me; and to the man for whom I do just about everything, Byron Bebergal. I write in memory of Ruth Bebergal and Eric Bebergal. Thank you, Scott, for this faithful friendship. Thanks to my son, Sam, truly the best person I have ever known. But finally, were it not for the home and hearth that my wife, Amy, gives me, I would be less than half the man I am. You are the backbone of this book. I love you.

A NOTE ON THE AUTHORS

PETER BEBERGAL graduated from Brandeis University and Harvard Divinity School. His essays, stories, and interviews have appeared in *Salon*, *Nextbook*, *Beliefnet*, the *Believer*, and the *Boston Globe*. Peter lives with his wife and son in Cambridge, Massachusetts.

SCOTT KORB received his undergraduate degree from the University of Wisconsin and graduate degrees from Union Seminary and Columbia University. He has written for *Harper's*, *Gastronomica*, the *Revealer*, *Commonweal*, and *Killing the Buddha*. He lives in Brooklyn, New York.